Acknowledgements

I have many people to thank for helping me write this book. Ann Greatrex, social work administrator at Keele University, for shielding me from some of the claims on my time as programme director of the BA (Hons) Social Work programme. Charlotte Williams (University of Melbourne), for encouraging me to write this book in the first place. Zoe Parrott, for allowing me the use of her MA dissertation on discretion in social work. Alan McGauley (Sheffield Hallam University) and Elaine Power (Queen's University, Kingston, Ontario), for useful advice and information; not forgetting the anonymous reviewer who made many helpful suggestions when reviewing the book. Finally, I wish to acknowledge my students for their interest and patience when I tried out some of the ideas developed in this book.

SOCIAL WORK AND POVERTY
A critical approach

Lester Parrott

First published in Great Britain in 2014 by

Policy Press
University of Bristol
6th Floor
Howard House
Queen's Avenue
Clifton
Bristol BS8 1SD
UK
t: +44 (0)117 331 5020
f: +44 (0)117 331 5369
pp-info@bristol.ac.uk
www.policypress.co.uk

North America office:
Policy Press
c/o The University of Chicago Press
1427 East 60th Street
Chicago, IL 60637, USA
t: +1 773 702 7700
f: +1 773 702 9756
sales@press.uchicago.edu
www.press.uchicago.edu

© Policy Press 2014

British Library Cataloguing in Publication Data
A catalogue record for this book is available from the British Library

Library of Congress Cataloging-in-Publication Data
A catalog record for this book has been requested

ISBN 978 1 44730 794 5 paperback
ISBN 978 1 44730 795 2 hardcover

Cover design by Qube Design Associates, Bristol
Front cover image: www.alamy.com
Printed and bound in Great Britain by CPI Group (UK) Ltd, Croydon, CR0 4YY
Policy Press uses environmentally responsible print partners.

Contents

Preface

I am writing this preface at a time when the issue of welfare, or social security as it used to be called, is receiving banner headlines in the press and on television. The Minister for Work and Pensions, Iain Duncan Smith (salary £134,565 per year), claimed he could live on £53 Income Support per week if he had to (*Daily Telegraph*, 2013), although he refused to do so when challenged by campaigners against 'welfare reform'. Duncan Smith is married to Betsy Fremantle, the daughter of the 5th Baron Cottesloe, their children were sent to Eton and they live in Lord Cottesloe's 17th-century Old House in the village of Swanbourne in Buckinghamshire. And he tells us he knows what it is like to be unemployed because when he left the Scots Guards, he had to look for employment.

The popular press reports that a mother and father on long-term Income Support, who conspired to set their house on fire and in the process accidentally killed their six children, are headline news as the 'Vile product of Welfare UK' (*Daily Mail*, 2013). George Osborne, Chancellor of the Exchequer, has climbed onto the bandwagon, calling for further questioning of the level of benefits paid to claimants with large families.

These headlines that emerge on a regular basis in the popular press create a climate of ignorance, fear and suspicion about the vast majority of people who legitimately rely on social security for their daily existence, and this includes around six million working families claiming Working Families Tax Credit. These stories have an effect. A recent Trades Union Congress (TUC) poll, conducted by TUC/YouGov (2012), showed that on average people think that 41 per cent of the entire welfare budget goes on benefits to unemployed people, whereas the true figure is actually only 3 per cent. The poll identified three groups of respondents, moving from the least knowledgeable to those with moderate understanding to those with the best knowledge about welfare benefits. Respondents felt that 27 per cent of the welfare budget was claimed fraudulently, while the government's own figure is 0.7 per cent. Further findings showed that those respondents who were the least knowledgeable regarding social security were the most hostile, for example, 71 per cent of those less knowledgeable thought welfare had created a culture of dependency. In addition, more than half (53 per cent) of those most knowledgeable thought that benefits were too generous.

It is my personal view that in the current climate almost anybody claiming social security benefit is seen as a potential 'scrounger'. People with disabilities and those who are unemployed (and soon, those in employment claiming Universal Credit) are subject to a range of controls and tests as to their entitlement to claim benefits, sending the message that we must be constantly vigilant to prevent the 'system' being cheated. Yet the present government is reducing the upper rate of income tax, has done little to curb the bonus culture within the financial services sector, is allowing energy companies that mislead their customers into paying higher energy bills to be fined derisory amounts and is apparently unable to ensure that some multinational companies, such as Google and Starbucks, pay even the minimum amount of tax for which they are legally required to do so. This disparity in the treatment of the poor compared to the rich and powerful is no better illustrated than in the focus on social security fraud and tax evasion.

Her Majesty's Revenue & Customs' (HMRC) criminal investigations department now has 2,222 staff; its specialist investigations department, which looks at corporate tax avoidance and the use of offshore arrangements, comprises 1,424 staff. Compare this to the Department for Work and Pensions staff numbering 3,250 who are actively engaged in social security fraud investigation. Comparing these numbers between the two agencies, the numbers are roughly similar and apparently unproblematic, until you look at the disparity in the amount of income lost through tax evasion compared to benefit fraud. In 2011/12 £1.2 billion of total benefit expenditure was overpaid due to fraud, while in 2012 HMRC calculated the tax gap, that is, the difference between the money they did collect and what they should have collected, to be £32 billion (HMRC, 2012). Although similar numbers of staff operate within the two agencies, the revenue lost to tax avoidance is some 32 times greater!

This book is designed to redress this imbalance of perspective, and considers the evidence that is available about the nature of poverty in the UK and the reality of living on low wages and/or social security. It is intended to help social workers and anybody else who reads this book to think constructively about how best to work with people who live in poverty. I make no apologies for stating at times in this book what social workers ought to do to combat the poverty that service users face, because I believe that social work is a moral and a practical activity, which implies that practice must be informed by a clear ethical perspective based on social justice. I hope that having read this book people will feel a sense of injustice and anger at how people living in poverty are treated. From a personal viewpoint, I hope social workers and the student social workers I teach will channel this anger in a constructive way to help eliminate poverty in this country.

Introduction

This is a book that looks at the nature of social work and poverty within the United Kingdom (UK). However, it mostly draws on experiences from England, as the delivery of social security policy has not been devolved to Wales, Northern Ireland and Scotland, and therefore similar issues will affect those devolved governments. Many of the experiences that are highlighted here will no doubt find echoes with readers from other parts of the globe, and I hope they will find something of interest.

Social workers work with many different kinds of people, the majority of whom are poor. Poverty nearly always characterises the experience of being a service user and is often correlated with the problems that people present to social work departments. Those requiring the help of a social worker, having experienced domestic violence (Humphreys, 2007) or a mental health problem (Gould, 2006), are more likely to be living in poverty. People who voluntarily seek the help of social workers have usually exhausted all other avenues of help. In a capitalist society such as the UK, a premium is placed on people's own coping capacity and increasingly the expectation that they use their own resources to cope with their problems, even when the genesis of these problems are social rather than individual. Requiring help from others may mean that these people feel they have failed in some way. And the nature of the help that is offered can often reinforce this feeling of failure when the organisations charged with alleviating poverty seek to control and sometimes even punish those seeking their help.

The social security system is undergoing a significant change through the Welfare Reform Act 2012 (WRA 2012), part of which requires unemployed people tolerating more stringent tests in assessing their jobseeking behaviour; people with long-standing disabilities are also being assessed as to their ability to work. If they fail such tests, then their benefit may be withdrawn or reduced significantly.

Social workers are therefore working in a harsher environment for those who are poor. Their room for manoeuvre in seeking help for such service users is increasingly constrained. Social workers' caseloads and working conditions can also militate against effective engagement with issues of poverty. The combined pressures on service users and social workers alike may therefore make countering the effects of poverty a daunting, but not an impossible, task.

The aims and objectives of this book are to explore and critically engage with the issue of poverty as experienced by social workers and service users. Chapter 1 places the issue of poverty within a historical context, taking the reader from the beginnings of poor relief, as it was known, to the Poor Law (Amendment) Act 1834, the reform of the Poor Law and the emergence of the welfare state. It explores the links between the Poor Law (Amendment) Act 1834 and the current configuration of social security policy in respect to the WRA 2012. It identifies some of the recurrent themes that obstruct the endeavours of social workers and service users to counter the effects of poverty, in particular, ideas that single out the 'deserving' from the 'undeserving' poor, the reinforcement of work discipline and the concept of less eligibility. These ideas have been used to control and punish people living in poverty, particularly in periods of high unemployment. The result for service users is that they can be easily stigmatised and considered less deserving of help due to their implied laziness or immorality.

Chapter 2 considers the concept of poverty, exploring some basic definitions, considering how poverty is measured and exploring the range of theories employed to understand and explain why there are significant numbers of people living in poverty in the UK. These definitions and theories are explored in relation to social workers' engagement with people experiencing poverty. It is argued that social workers need to understand how their perception of such definitions and theories has an impact on their practice and the lives of the service users they seek to help.

Chapter 3 looks in greater depth at the current Coalition government's policies towards people in poverty, in particular, exploring the implications of the WRA 2012 for service users. In analysing this legislation it is argued that social workers need to become more aware of welfare rights issues.

Chapter 4 builds on the impact of the current Coalition government's policies to look at the experience of poverty from a service user's perspective. Drawing on the testimonies of those living in poverty from across the globe, it argues that social workers must understand such experiences, especially feelings of stigma and shame. In addition, it explores service users' experience of social work intervention in this area, and critically reflects on how social workers can begin to respond to the needs of service users more effectively. It argues that to counter poverty, social work must listen to service users' generally negative experiences of social work services.

Chapter 5 takes the narratives of people living in poverty to explore how social workers can engage effectively with issues of poverty. In particular, it considers the importance of addressing issues of anti-oppressive practice (AOP). It draws on examples to look at how social workers can address the poverty of service users, and links theories of AOP with an active engagement with poverty from the perspective of the practice of social workers, placing this within a wider social context.

Chapter 6 investigates the organisational and service delivery issues in relation to social work services, and argues that the way such services are organised has an impact on how poverty is experienced by service users. In this regard social work departments as an organisational practice are considered as both part of the problem in reinforcing poverty and as the solution in reordering priorities towards people living in poverty.

Chapter 7 briefly presents some of the evidence in relation to the different social divisions present in society, analysing how the impact and experience of poverty is related to difference and diversity. Relevant research is considered in relation to how poverty may be experienced differently through the experience of such social divisions as 'race', gender and class. These different experiences are then related to a number of issues not usually covered in texts on poverty, including access to food, obesity, problematic drug use and child abuse and neglect.

Chapter 8 places poverty and social work within a global context. It looks at global poverty and relates this to social work intervention with different groups of people who migrate to the UK, including those people seeking asylum, migrants seeking work and people trafficked into the UK. Social work practice is then considered in the light of these global challenges.

The final concluding chapter draws on some of the key themes developed in the book, and outlines the main areas of engagement for social workers wishing to end poverty in the UK.

1

Poverty and social work:
the historical context

Research on the attitudes of social work practitioners and students provides a mixed view of how poverty is understood. An early study by Becker (1997) argued that social workers had an attenuated view of poverty, holding largely discriminatory views of how people became poor and operating from mostly individualistic theories to understand service users' experiences of poverty. Theories that understood poverty as a structural problem were less likely to emerge in social workers' accounts, which in turn had a negative impact on what social workers considered appropriate in terms of their practice. As Davis and Wainwright (2005) observed, social workers' attitudes could be considered ambivalent, confused and at the extreme, hostile to service users living in poverty. Considering the current organisation of social work, where services are not attuned to issues of poverty, the consequences for service users can be highly negative. Thus current social work practice, centred on legal and procedural concerns, may result in social work ignoring action to combat the effects of poverty in service users' lives.

Why is it, then, that despite all the evidence that points to the preponderance of service users living in poverty (Schorr, 1992; Becker, 1997; Dowling, 1999), so little is done to counter it by social workers?

In order to understand this phenomenon we need to explore how poverty has historically been addressed in the UK. In particular, we need to understand how social work as it has developed never saw itself as the appropriate medium through which the provision of assistance to those living in poverty should pass.

The origins of public assistance to the poor in the UK can be traced back to the succession of Poor Laws instituted over time that governed the way in which poor relief, as it was known, could be administered. (The development of the Poor Laws took different trajectories in Scotland and Ireland, albeit influenced by similar principles as they emerged in England.) The Poor Laws were not the only form of assistance to people living in poverty; the provision of relief also involved the church and private charities. Many charities were often influenced by deeply held religious convictions to intervene in the lives of poor people (Fielder, 2006). Much of the earlier provisions to people experiencing poverty were localised, based on the parish as the unit of administration. This was a reflection of the largely rural nature of the UK and its economy in which control over the Poor Law was in the hands of local magistrates. This form of giving saw assistance to poor people more as a gift of charity and benevolence in which the better off in society had a duty to help those people living in poverty whom they considered to be their social and moral inferiors. A lifetime of poverty was seen as the natural state for the majority of the population.

Once industrial capitalism began to develop, assistance became less communal and more individualised, as the new entrepreneurial class became more critical of the wastefulness, as they viewed it, of the old systems of giving. It is from this moment that assistance to poor people began to be dominated by attitudes that emphasised individualism and self-help. Poverty was understood as a moral problem, a scourge on society brought about by a morally degenerate underclass or residuum (Kidd, 1999). From their inception the Poor Laws were always considered to be a last resort for the destitute poor, while poverty itself was seen as the natural state for the majority. Thus many charities' efforts were directed at preventing the poor from sinking into destitution or pauperism, as it was called. This became more evident after the Poor Law (Amendment) Act 1834 that paired back the relatively generous levels of assistance that had characterised earlier periods.

Poverty before capitalism

As Novak (1988) argues, the treatment of the able-bodied poor prior to the rise of industrial capitalism in the late 18th century can be described as an attempt to contain and control those people living in poverty within the locales of a rural society. This involved limiting the movement of labour around the country and punishing those deemed to be idle and not in work. The landed ruling class was concerned to maintain their hold over the poor as a means to store a pool of labour available to work in the agricultural economy. As capitalism rose to prominence in an emerging industrialised society, and the importance of a money economy to people's existence began to grow, so the social relations that had characterised the rural economy increasingly became a fetter on the movement of labour around the country. Thus a more coherent response was required if poor people were to be contained. Ultimately, by the reign of Elizabeth I, a compulsory poor rate was levied on property owners within the parishes to provide relief for those who could not work. In addition, Justices of the Peace were required to purchase materials that would enable the able-bodied poor to be put to work. These provisions were later codified in the Poor Law 1601. As the century progressed, it became clear that society was caught between an existing ruling class based on the ownership of land trying to manage the problem of people experiencing poverty, in the face of a burgeoning class of merchants and nascent factory owners in the cities, who were requiring a more flexible approach to the problem of poverty.

The landed classes faced an increasing challenge from a capitalist class that required greater freedom to exploit the labour of the rural working class. While from the point of view of capital poor people could be contained in the country through the administration of the local Poor Law, the 'rights' of the urban property owners to exploit the labour of those people living in poverty was stifled. The outcome of this conflict between the landed aristocracy and the urbanised capital class over control of people living in poverty was to be further regulation of poor relief. This resulted in a regime of relief that was designed to weaken the Elizabethan Poor Law in order to contain the cost of poor relief, encouraging a greater freedom for labour and encouraging migration to the centres of employment in the towns and cities. However, the aims of the urbanised capitalist class were modified by the still powerful hold that the landed aristocracy had over Parliament, and therefore the legislation that developed represented a compromise between these two standpoints.

The shift in emphasis is often understood as the change from what some writers have called one of a moral economy to deal with the problem of poverty to one embodied in a free market economy. Thus the old order emphasised, to an extent, its duty to support people living in poverty in a limited way in a society in which the rich and poor, the landed and the property-less, were fixed within a rigid hierarchy of social relations (Polanyi, 1957; Thompson, 1968). The free market economy emphasised the rights of those who owned property to be able to exploit this in the way they saw fit. Within this, the labourers owned their property, that is, labour, and it was up to the labourers to support themselves through the selling of this labour power. It was the right of the owner of the means of production, those who owned the land and the machines on which the labourer would toil, to buy this labour at the most economical price. This is not to say that this was a purely economic argument in terms of efficiency, but it also acquired moral justification, that is, the freedom of the factory owner to develop their business to produce profit and the freedom of the labourer as an autonomous individual to sell their labour power. From this point of view the capitalist owed nothing to the labourer except his wages, and held no duty or responsibility towards others except themselves. The nature of social relations was then to be transformed from clearly defined duties and responsibilities to a seemingly fluid set of relationships tied only by the impersonal laws of contract. As Dean (2002) observes, the development of the Poor Law reinforced the principle that any form of social assistance was to be provided on a discretionary basis; social assistance has never been a social right, and as such, informs the treatment of poverty to this day.

Reform of the Poor Law

The social upheavals underway by the late 18th century created a new set of social relations in society, and these changes provided the context for the reform of the Poor Law. The relatively static systems of regulation of those people living in poverty were increasingly coming under strain. The gradual move of the population from the countryside to the city, and the financial aftermath of funding the war against France, resulted in serious economic and social distress and significant unrest in the early 1800s. Handloom weavers in Lancashire destroyed the new machines that had made them redundant as new technology drove down the price of the production of cotton. In the countryside the 'Captain Swing' riots resulted in rural labourers burning hayricks and assaulting the local gentry in protest against the increasing levels of rural unemployment. The cost of poor relief began to increase significantly as a response by the landed classes to the rising levels of rural poverty and unrest. These responses took the form of relief through subsidising wages in the rural economy (for example, the Speenhamland System, a system that subsidised farm labourers' wages in line with the price of bread) and the use of public works to provide employment. The rise in the cost of relief to the poor brought forth a critical response of the existing system. One influential critic was Thomas Malthus, who, in his work *An essay on the principle of population, as it affects the future improvement of society* (Malthus, [1806] 1989), argued that the increase in population outstripped the ability to provide the means to maintain its subsistence. In particular, he posited that poor relief was undermining the independence of labourers. Generous Poor Law provision encouraged the growth of population within those classes least able to support such increases. Thus, he argued that the Poor Laws created increasing numbers of the poor who in turn required extra poor relief to maintain them. For Malthus the dangers were clear in that independently minded labourers would be dragged down to the level of the irresponsible poor on poor relief; the problem was not poverty as such, but the destitute who were maintained by the Poor Law rather than forced to seek employment. Dependent poverty was morally wrong, a vice that had to be expunged from society. Malthus's prescription for change was the wholesale repeal of the Poor Laws rather than reform. Malthus died in the same year that the Poor Law was amended, and his essay had by that time run to six subsequent editions. Although Malthus had made much impact in his critique of the Poor Laws, his prescription was not carried forward into the subsequent reform.

The amendment of the Poor Law was brought on by the impact of the hard winter of 1829 that caused a harshening of economic conditions for the poor and a hardening response from the magistrates charged with administering poor relief. The 'Captain Swing' revolt of agricultural labourers, mainly in the South East of England, was a consequence of rising levels of rural unemployment and inadequate levels of outdoor relief paid. The rioters asserted their right to decent levels of relief to support them through such hard times. This revolt was threatening to the local landed classes who feared further insurrection if these demands were allowed to spread.

In response to these concerns, Parliament instituted a full-scale review of the Poor Laws by setting up a Royal Commission on the Poor Laws in 1832 charged with investigating the existing operation of poverty relief and then to develop policies to reform them. The key figures within the Commission were Edwin Chadwick, Secretary to the Poor Law Commission, and Nassau Senior, a political economist with an unshakeable faith in laissez-faire economics. Chadwick, who ultimately wrote the report, was therefore in a powerful position to steer the outcome of the Commission's findings. He was a believer in the ideas of Jeremy Bentham, whose utilitarian philosophy had had a huge impact on the intellectual climate of the 19th century. For Chadwick, any policy devised to change the Poor Law should be considered in the light of the utilitarian concept of the greatest happiness for the greatest number of people within a society. This required not the abolition of the Poor Laws, as Malthus had argued, but for a refinement in which mechanisms could be devised to achieve this ultimate utilitarian goal. As a starting point the Commission was at pains to distinguish between the able-bodied poor and those called the indigent or pauper who relied on poor relief. Poor Law reform should separate the two groups so that only the indigent, consisting of the impotent poor —children, widows, older people – should be offered relief as it had been configured before. The able-bodied pauper and his family were to be subject to more stringent tests. Thus the test applied one of 'less eligibility' in which the able-bodied pauper should not be given relief in excess of what the employed labouring poor could earn in wages. The principle of 'less eligibility' was then buttressed by a further deterrent to pauperism by only offering relief to the able-bodied pauper inside the workhouse. Conditions in the workhouse should test the pauper's resolve, so that diets were poor, families segregated from one another, males from females, and strict discipline and labour was the order of the day to educate the pauper into habits of hard work and industry. The key issue for the reformers was to ensure that the able-bodied labouring poor were separated from the able-bodied paupers so that the habits of thrift and industry could be maintained, unsullied by the 'idle and feckless' pauper. If the new Poor Law could act as a symbol of dread, so much the better, so that only the most desperate would enter the gates of the workhouse. The overriding assumption underpinning this approach was that poverty was a voluntary and therefore reversible condition. The solution to poverty was the belief in the beneficence of the free market, by which the unemployed labourer would be returned to employment once demand for his labour had recovered.

The Poor Law (Amendment) Act 1834

The Royal Commission on the Poor Laws commenced in 1832 and collected information from 26 assistant commissioners, each appointed to investigate a particular district's management of the old Poor Law. The brief for the commissioners was to investigate the 'evils' perpetrated by the old system. Not surprisingly, the vast amount of information gleaned enabled Chadwick and Senior to construct a report that chimed with Senior's virulent opposition to the old system and Chadwick's conviction that a new system needed to be developed from utilitarian principles (Brundage, 2002). The subsequent legislation represented the beginning of a centralised system of poor relief. Poor Law commissioners were charged with oversight of the Act and required to report to Parliament. The 1834 legislation restructured the local system of poor relief based on the parish by organising parishes into Poor Law unions. The unions would be responsible for operating a workhouse overseen by elected boards of guardians and administered by paid officials. The Poor Law Commission had limited powers to standardise systems of administration, to prevent certain kinds of fraud and to veto officials who were deemed unsuitable. However, the new Poor Law was not comprehensive in its coverage and was excluded from interfering in certain parishes and unions set up under the Gilbert Act 1782; it was not until the 1860s that the Poor Law commissioners could wield their power across the whole of the country when the metropolitan boroughs were finally subsumed under its administration (Englander, 1998).

In its focus on poor people the objective was to ensure that the distressed, able-bodied labourer should always be required to seek work at whatever level of pay, rather than seek relief. The principle of less eligibility therefore ensured that only the most desperate of labourers would seek poor relief. When relief was given, the intention was that this should only be offered within a workhouse. However, the practice of offering indoor relief was hampered by the slowness of some unions to build workhouses. Where workhouses were built, it was found that when sharp rises in unemployment were experienced, there was pressure on finding places inside the workhouse for all those who qualified. As a consequence, the workhouse principle was virtually undermined before it had begun. In effect, outdoor relief continued to be paid, but subject to the recipient working in the workhouse labour yards when the workhouse could not accommodate all the unemployed who qualified for relief.

An additional barrier faced by unemployed labourers searching for work was the settlement rules. These provisions required that labourers had to be maintained not where they resided but in their place of settlement (by birth or marriage), and had to return there if they required relief. This process of removal was a constant worry – some unions, where it was deemed cheaper to provide relief rather than remove the pauper, did so, but the fear of removal remained.

The outcome of the Poor Law Commission's work was to ensure that the Poor Law would be reformed to further the interests of the rising class of capitalists who were beginning to dominate the debate on the Act. This did not mean that they had complete control, but they were beginning to mount a serious challenge against the landed interests. This challenge was further enhanced by many middle-class males acquiring the vote through the Reform Act 1832. The reform of the Poor Law seemed to satisfy both parties in that by reforming the Poor Law rural unrest could be quashed, as Chadwick had emphasised in his report that labourers had a right to a fair subsistence (Kidd, 1999). In enforcing less eligibility it in part spoke to the supporters of the free market in affirming the necessity for people living in poverty to labour at any price and at the same time encourage a national market for labour. Thus surplus rural labourers could be 'encouraged' to look for work in the smoky factories of the Midlands and the North, while ensuring for the urban ratepayers that unemployed labourers who fell onto the parish for relief could be returned to their place of birth through the settlement provisions of the new Act. Although these provisions seem contradictory, freeing labour to look for work while returning labourers to their place of birth if they wished to claim relief, it did make sense for the urban ratepayers who had the benefit of a free market in labour but not the responsibility to support the labourer if he became unemployed.

Consequences of the Poor Law (Amendment) Act 1834

For the authors of the Act the outcomes were deemed a spectacular success; in 1834 poor relief cost £6.5 million, but by 1837 it had fallen to just over £4 million (Brundage, 2002). Throughout the rest of the century the cost of poor relief never rose beyond £6 million per annum. For those boards of guardians who administered the new regime with enthusiasm, however, they were to be confronted with public outcry at the brutality of the new regime. *The Times* ran a series of campaigns to moderate the operation of the Poor Law. In a particularly notorious case in a workhouse in Andover, inmates were found to be malnourished as a consequence of the eager application of less eligibility. Thus, in periods of economic downturn, when the number of labourers seeking work rose, the level of wages became depressed to an extent that subsistence could be put in jeopardy. If the principle of less eligibility was to be rigidly adhered to, those in the workhouses would be living below the level of subsistence. However, if the authors of the Poor Law congratulated themselves, they would not have been so content with how this legislation was received by the working masses. The poet John Clare, who became famous in the 1830s, had been a former pauper and wrote scathingly of how the new workhouse system had had an impact on the rural landscape:

> These were the times that plainness must regret
> These were the times that labour feels as yet
> Ere mock'd improvements plans enclose the moor
> And farmers build a workhouse for the poor.

> (John Clare, 1601-03, quoted in Charlesworth, 2001)

Throughout England and Wales there were violent protests against its operation. The Rebecca Riots in Wales, for example, led to attacks on workhouses that slowed their construction, with 10 unions as late as 1858 still without such a facility. Some local unions in England also hindered the development of the legislation where employer opposition to the strictness of the regime led to a less draconian system being employed. For example, as Kidd (1999) points out, in Rochdale workhouses operated more as almshouses. Thus, in terms of its operation, although there was an element of centralised authority, there was much room for local discretion in how the system was operating. For those workers who had a modicum of spare income, rebellion was replaced by attempts to circumvent the Poor Law altogether by paying into Friendly Societies whereby slightly better off workers could insure themselves, to a degree, against becoming unemployed, and receive benefits in times of want. This alternative was only available to those with a consistent source of income from which they could pay their weekly dues. Mann (1992) observes that by 1872, Friendly Societies had some four million members, but for the poorest workers, the Poor Law or charity was the only recourse in times of want.

For those forced to call on the Poor Law for help, paupers feared the process and consequences. Those entering the workhouse lost any rights to vote, affecting those few middle-class males forced into claiming relief during hard times. Working-class males were unaffected as they did not acquire the vote until later on in the century. The poor diets, monotonous hard work and strict discipline left little time for any other pursuits; older people rightly feared dying in the workhouse, not only fearing a pauper's unmarked grave but as a result of the Anatomy Act 1832, their bodies could be given over to medical schools for dissection (Englander, 1998). The harshness of the regime and the subsequent shame attached to entering the workhouse that became a mark of personal failure left a huge impression on all those who would come into contact with the privations of the workhouse.

As such, the workhouse and the Poor Law institution left a constant reminder to working people that any failure to support themselves could lead to the shame and degradation that awaited them inside the workhouse. The workhouse entered the popular culture of the time, with many songs and poems all highlighting the dreadful treatment awaiting the pauper in the workhouse. For example, Albert Chevalier, a music hall artist of the early 20th century, became famous for his rendition of 'My Dear Old Dutch'. Chevalier would be on stage, depicted against the backdrop of the workhouse gates. The song told the story of Chevalier as an older man singing about his love for his wife (his 'Dutch' of the song title), the implication being that they were about to be separated as they entered the workhouse. The audience would have instantly recognised what was happening, even though the song itself never mentions the workhouse.

The Poor Law and charity

As the 19th century unfolded, the authority of the newly centralised Poor Law administration asserted its legitimacy over the recalcitrant Poor Law unions. The reform of the Poor Law had not initially pleased many sections of society. Certainly the riots of poor people were testament to their opposition, but the emerging capitalist factory owners also found much that was wanting in the legislation, particularly around the issue of reducing outdoor relief. In other areas, where the problem of unemployed paupers was not an issue, many unions simply ignored the existence of the Act and continued in their own way of relieving poverty (Englander, 1998.). However, the stresses and strains of the developing economic system and rapid urbanisation as a result of increased capitalist development in the cities led to significant pressures on the financing of the Poor Law. The Settlement Acts were undermined by legislation that allowed widows and children resident for five years in a parish to receive poor relief from that parish and not to be returned. Thus, as populations moved to the cities, the strain of financing those areas where large numbers of the poor lived began to tell. This culminated in the Union Chargeability Act 1865 that required wealthier parishes to contribute out of their rates to the poorer parishes. The problems experienced in London were also recognised by the Metropolitan Poor Act 1867 that established a Common

Poor Fund, requiring each union in the city to contribute to a fund for the construction and maintenance of workhouses. The Poor Law Board also acquired new powers to nominate their own members to the London guardians to counter what was considered the laxness of administration by some guardians, particularly in their generous approach to giving relief.

Although for many enthusiasts the new Poor Law was expected to remain as the most effective weapon in the fight to develop independence in the able-bodied labourer, the 1860s were to severely test their optimism. In London a series of relief crises caused severe hardship among workers. Disorder, rioting and looting followed as the Poor Law unions struggled to cope with the increase in poor relief applications. As recourse to poor relief became harder, added pressure was felt by local charities that tried to cope with the flood of applications from those made destitute. The expansion of charitable relief was seen as anathema by the supporters of the Poor Law, warning that an indiscriminate outpouring of charity would undermine the independence of the able-bodied pauper. As Stedman Jones (1984) outlines, this created a fear in the middle classes that poor people as a group would be permanently outcast from respectable society in which the principles of independence and self-help would disappear from the character of those people living in poverty.

Coupled with the London riots throughout the 1860s was the economic crisis in the Lancashire cotton industry as a result of the 'cotton famine'. When the supply of raw cotton dried up as a result of the American Civil War and the economic embargo enforced by the Unionist North on the Confederate South, thousands of cotton workers were laid off. The impact, as in London, of many thousands of workers asking for relief in the cotton districts was to throw the Lancashire unions into chaos. As the Poor Law failed to cope, charities again stepped in to provide some help, coordinated through a Central Relief Committee. As Kidd (1999) has argued, neither charity nor the Poor Law unions could cope with the increase in destitution. The result was a further loosening of the workhouse principle in the Public Works (Manufacturing Districts) Act 1863, which provided cheap loans to local authorities to employ redundant workers in public works.

As the economic crisis worsened in the 1860s, so the response of the supporters of the Poor Law was to argue that the founding principles of the 1834 Act had been undermined by the blurring of charity with the Poor Law. They argued that the giving of charitable relief to those who would normally have been dealt with by the workhouse was undermining the distinction between the 'deserving' and 'undeserving' poor. The spectre of the clever able-bodied pauper being able to exploit the generosity of the charitable bodies and claim poor relief loomed large in their view. The idea that outdoor relief could be paid in aid of wages had to be halted. The cure was to reaffirm the role of the workhouse and to create a clear distinction between the Poor Law and charity. The Goschen Minute 1869, issued by the President of the Local Government Board (Lord Goschen), which had superseded the Poor Law board, aimed to stem the flow of indiscriminate relief. The tenor of the Minute was to urge a clear division between the Poor Law in dealing with pauperism and the role of charities in providing relief for those in danger of falling into pauperism. By this measure it was hoped to restore the operation of the Poor Law to deterring pauperism and to reduce outdoor relief, that in Goschen's view was spiralling out of control. In the same year that the Goschen Minute was circulated, the Society for Organising Charitable Relief and Repressing Mendacity (COS, Charity Organization Society) was formed to coordinate the operations of charitable giving, first in London, then later spreading out to the major cities such as Manchester and Nottingham. The principles informing the COS were also influential in founding similar organisations in Australia and the US. The COS represented an approach to helping those people living in poverty through the application of what was considered the scientific investigation and analysis of an applicant's character, and in turn offering practical guidance. This had been present, for example, among local statistical societies formed in many Victorian towns to gather facts about poverty and from organisations such as the Workhouse Visiting Society, which not only provided charity to workhouse inmates, but also collected information on the conditions inside the workhouse. A similar approach had also been developed by Thomas Chalmers in 1819 in Glasgow and was characterised by close examination of an individual's circumstances, with a view to providing practical help and moral guidance (Pierson, 2011).

The help provided by the COS was established firmly within the principles informing the Poor Law. The aim was to provide advice and guidance to those considered 'deserving' cases who were in danger of falling into the workhouse. In order for this to be effected, a rigorous analysis of an individual or family's condition needed to be carried out to avoid the clever pauper from benefiting from the help given. Investigation of the person's home circumstances was vital in assessing the 'deservingness' of the individual. Once desert had been established, then the application of casework was seen as the best method. Many of the 'caseworkers' were drawn from the middle classes and were in most cases women. Visiting poor people provided an outlet for participation in public service normally denied to women by the patriarchal attitudes of Victorian society that expected middle-class women to be homemakers, to which it was argued their character was best suited.

In entering into casework with people living in poverty the visitors were practising a nascent form of social work. Each case had to be investigated individually and then, if help was required, this was sought from appropriate individuals either willing to give help in kind or to provide more direct forms of help such as writing letters to hospitals to access treatment. It is important to note that the 'help' provided through casework was not to be drawn from a common fund but had to be procured for each individual case. In this way it was hoped to avoid a common recourse to indiscriminate help and to tailor an appropriate individual response. Any help that was given should be temporary and reformatory to restore the applicant to independence. The influence of the caseworker was also important. The intention was that through experiencing the proximity of their betters as 'role models', the poor would be inspired to develop habits of independence and self-help. Relationships between the helper and the helped should be non-familiar and distant lest the helper became too much entangled in the lives of those they were helping. There was the sense, as Jones (1983) has argued, that contamination might accrue, in which those habits of moral probity exemplified by the middle-class visitor could be undermined by association with the inferior morality of poor people. Casework was seen as a scientific activity that required visitors to be carefully selected and then trained in its techniques. This culminated in 1896 with the establishment of the first training scheme for social workers, and by 1913 it had developed into a full-blown training course organised by the London School of Economics and Political Science (Woodroofe, 1962).

The COS was the dominant force in charitable activity for 50 years after its foundation in 1869 (Powell, 2001). The deformation of character as the key to understanding the cause of poverty promulgated by the COS was about to be challenged. The recognition that forces beyond an individual's character rooted in the malfunctioning of society began to gain a foothold. Canon Barnett, a prominent member of the COS, began to argue that poverty needed to be addressed by the state, and that charity of itself would be insufficient to deal with such social factors as unemployment which caused so much distress to the able-bodied poor. Barnett founded the Settlement Movement that aimed to provide a different approach to the problem of poverty. The Settlement Movement began in London in 1884 but spread to other cities such as Birmingham and Nottingham and was an attempt to develop a stronger link between the middle classes and people experiencing poverty. This was thought possible by encouraging educated young people drawn from the major universities to go and live among poor people. Their role through the provision of their example and providing practical help in the community, coupled with the promotion of social reform, reflected an understanding of poverty that moved somewhat from blaming the poor for their condition.

Socialists and trade unionists all became active in the later part of the 19th century, and began to lobby for a change in the way poverty was treated and in particular, for a full-scale abolition of the Poor Law. The agitation against the Poor Law was also echoed in the way that successive governments in the late 19th century had loosened the controls on outdoor relief for the able-bodied unemployed; for example, in 1886 a Conservative government had allowed local councils to provide public works schemes to ameliorate levels of unemployment. By the turn of the 20th century a strong groundswell of pressure had built to reform if not remove the Poor Law from the statute books. The newly formed Labour Party (1905), alongside an increasingly vocal trade union movement, put their support behind changing the system. As a result, another Commission of the Poor Law 1905-09 was called to investigate its operation and to advise on reform. This was seen by those supporters of the COS view as an opportunity to redress the way that the Poor Law had been undermined by government policy, particularly towards the unemployed, and to return it to its original principles.

For socialists such as Beatrice Webb, who became a member of the Commission, this was an opportunity to do away with the Poor Law altogether and to replace it with something she argued would be more democratic and more efficient. The challenge to the operation and principles of the Poor Law were fuelled by the alternative explanations of poverty that were reflected in the terms of reference of the Commission. Its remit was to report on:

> Everything which appertains to … the problem of the poor, whether by their own fault , or by temporary lack of employment. (Englander, 1998, p 74)

The extent to which this shift in understanding had occurred can be partly explained by the campaigns mounted by the trade unions and socialists in highlighting the problems of unemployment, and also with the development in the late 19th century of social inquiry. Investigators such as Henry Mayhew, in *London Labour and the London poor* (1861), highlighted the inadequacy of earnings of those employed as labourers and the casual nature of employment for many which meant irregular earnings was a significant cause of poverty. Charles Booth, in *Life and labour of the people in London* (1889), focused on the East End of London and the casual employment within the docks there. His view was that the state should be involved in regulating the labour market to encourage the decasualisation of the docks that would lead to a certainty of income for the dock labourer. His concern was to ensure that the labouring classes should not be forced into the arms of the Poor Law. Indeed, he called for a clear demarcation between those he described as 'loafers' and 'idlers' unwilling to work, and the honest labourer. For the 'feckless', stronger remedies were called for by confining them into labour colonies and industrial homes where they could eventually be reformed or, if not, removed to the workhouse where they would wither away. He also called for non-contributory old age pensions that would reduce the competition for work to allow the true and honest labourer to be free of competition from older workers who may, he argued, be less efficient.

Although attitudes to poor people were still based on individualistic explanations, there was now an alternative constituency that began to campaign for action based on tackling the social conditions which caused poverty, or more radically by a few, such as the Social Democratic Federation, calling for the reordering of society away from a capitalist system which, they argued, created poverty (Jones, 1983). These positions can be characterised as below:

- Poverty is caused by the individual's lack of character and dependency on the state.
- Poverty is caused by inadequate social conditions such as unemployment, poor housing and lack of access to education.
- Poverty is caused by the unequal distribution of wealth and income in which a powerful minority are able, through their control of the key resources in society,

to use their power and influence to maintain their wealth at the expense of people living in poverty.

Summary

Why has this chapter focused on the Poor Law when this book is considering the relationship between social work and poverty? The relief of poverty was not just the preserve of the Poor Law but was also entwined with charities such as the COS and the churches that provided a significant amount of help to the poor. What is crucial to an understanding of how social work has treated poverty, however, is the separation of the able-bodied poor in employment and the able-bodied poor and the indigent. It is this second group of people with whom social work became and is still intimately involved. As the COS expanded its area of operation, the purpose of their efforts was to divert those considered deserving of help away from the clutches of the stigmatising Poor Law. The operations of the COS therefore represented the boundary between desert and punishment, charity and the Poor Law. Social work is therefore, to this day, reluctant to deal with the problems caused by poverty because in a way there is still the assumption that to be poor is not sufficient reason to require social work intervention. Social work deals with those who cannot deal with or tolerate their poverty. Those who find themselves in significant debt or those who, through other personal crises, are unable to manage their lives, have become the focal point of social work. It is only when a person exhibits problems other than poverty per se that the attention of social work is drawn to the poor. Therefore the links between poverty and these other problems are rarely drawn or seen as significant by social workers, as we shall see later. As Jones (1983) argues, social work has, through its individualistic casework tradition, seen poverty as a problem to be managed by individual service users rather than as a problem of the wider society in which social work operates. Under the previous Labour government much was made of the concept of 'social exclusion' (a concept closely associated with poverty), and a number of initiatives were developed to tackle this phenomenon. However, as Jordan (2007) argued, social work was kept organisationally apart from these initiatives, making a distinction between the task of social work in terms of child protection and mental health, for example, and the initiatives developed within communities to tackle social exclusion. Thus local authorities were organisationally separated from this project, seeing the programmes developed and the agencies responsible as distinct from local authority control.

Recommended reading

Novak, T. (1988) *Poverty and the state*, Milton Keynes: Open University Press.
Pierson, J. (2011) *Understanding social work: History and context*, Maidenhead: Open University Press.

2

Social work and the concept of poverty

This chapter considers some basic definitions of poverty and explores the range of theories employed to understand and explain why there are significant numbers of people living in poverty in the UK. These definitions and theories are explored in relation to social workers' engagement with poor people. Social workers need to understand how the use of such definitions and theories influence their practice and the lives of service users seeking their help.

We live in societies that are increasingly organised around the philosophy and practice of the marketplace. Governments and the media encourage us to see ourselves as individuals responsible for our own fate. In the UK the state increasingly expects that we make our own provision for those aspects of our life for which the state has in the past taken some degree of responsibility. In the realm of social work, more policy initiatives have been developed that encourage service users to become self-managing consumers of social work through, for example, the personalisation agenda. The organisation and delivery of services have progressively become outsourced to the private and independent sectors, and social workers themselves have become subject to more control over their practice through systems of managerial regulation. The pursuing of such policies has been designed to supervise the privatisation of social work services and the experiences of social workers and service users as they engage in the practical concerns of dealing with the social problems they confront. This system of marketisation and individualisation has been described as neo-liberalism:

> ... a theory of political economic practices that proposes that human well-being can best be advanced by liberating individual entrepreneurial freedoms and skills within an institutional framework characterized by strong private property rights, free markets and free trade. (Harvey, 2005, p 2)

This form of capitalism has become the dominant social system across the world, even in those former or current states that called themselves 'communist'. China, for example, has developed its own form of neo-liberalism within the context of a ruling Communist Party as it has embraced the market to generate economic growth (Harvey, 2005).

In calling neo-liberalism a social system it is important to evaluate its effects throughout society in general and its effect on individuals in particular. For Foucault (Chambon et al, 1999), on the one hand neo-liberal governments have sought to reduce the role and scope of government, but on the other have developed techniques for ensuring that individuals see themselves as individuals and not part of or connected to others within society. This has been characterised as the 'death of the social' (Rose, 1996a). In essence, individuals take responsibility for themselves so that problems that they may experience, such as poverty, are initially understood by them as their responsibility rather than problems that the state or wider society has some responsibility for. Thus social risks such as poverty are transformed into individual risks that can only be understood and dealt with through the self (see Rose, 1996a, 1996b; Moffat, 1999). The impact of these individualising ideas means that social workers are not immune from this individualising discourse and can be influenced like others in society. Although Foucault's position may not entirely explain such phenomena, it does provide a useful way of thinking about how issues such as poverty have become increasingly individualised. This can be understood from studies of social work students and social workers in terms of how they conceptualise poverty. Gilligan (2007) shows that the attitudes of social work students remain largely focused on individual explanations of social problems, such as poverty. Once students experience their social work course it is highly likely that they will not be exposed to much relevant training on the problems of poverty and social work (Davis and Wainwright, 2005). Monnickendam et al (2010), in reviewing the research to date, found strong similarities across countries such as the UK, US and Israel in that social work students preferred direct intervention at the individual and family level and were only moderately inclined to work with people living in poverty or work in more collective forms of practice. When Monnickendam et al (2010) conducted their own research in Israel with social work directors, they found that they did not perceive people experiencing poverty as a target population, were reluctant to work with poor clients and consequently failed to deliver services targeted at people living in poverty.

When social workers engage service users in their work, the attitudes and beliefs that they hold are crucial in enabling effective help. As Strier and Binyamin (2010) argue, the definitions and theories employed by social workers and their organisations determine the rationale for intervention in relation to poverty. For example, social work services that conceptualise poverty as a problem of and for the individual will lead to practice that tends to reflect these particular definitions and theories. In turn this will have particular consequences for service users in terms of the way in which the social worker interacts with them, but will also determine the kinds of solutions discussed and the services that may be available. Closely associated with individualistic approaches are those that focus on the culture, that is, the attitudes and beliefs of service users as implicated in poverty. Thus services that attempt to change what are considered to be the faulty norms and beliefs of service users are therefore more likely to be adopted.

This, in turn, has a significant impact on service users' feelings of stigma and their willingness to see social workers in a constructive light when they require help. Davies (2008) outlined the problems from a service user's perspective when explaining their reluctance to use services because of:

- the attitudes of the professional staff in the services that they found off-putting and patronising;
- thinking that services were not relevant to their needs;
- being ashamed of being in need or fearful of being judged as unable to cope;
- being worried about possible interference in their lives.

Exercise

In what ways do you think the ideas underpinning neo-liberalism and the attitudes of social workers reflect the historical legacy of the 19th-century view of capitalism and the attitudes of the COS towards people living in poverty?

If social workers want to work effectively alongside service users experiencing poverty, they need to think in ways that do not individualise the problem of poverty or engage in practice that reflects this. Social workers need to have a more informed understanding of the nature of poverty and in particular how it can be conceptualised. Individualistic conceptualisations of poverty generally lead to poor practice and the stigmatisation of service users; alternative social conceptualisations that can contribute to an anti-oppressive approach to poverty will be more effective (Strier and Binyamin, 2010).

The next section considers the conceptualisation of poverty.

Definitions

Poverty has been defined in two ways:

- Absolute poverty, defined as the absence of those items that sustain basic human functioning, usually confined to the basic physical needs of food, clothing and shelter.
- Relative poverty, a concept related to the changing economic development, customs and social practices of a society at a particular time. It accounts for what the majority of a population considers to be necessary to live a reasonable life in relation to the physical as well as social necessities that they understand as essential for their participation in society.

This juxtaposition of absolute against relative definitions is not as simple as it might seem. For example, Seebohm Rowntree, one of the first social investigators interested in defining poverty, has been associated with an absolute approach to poverty (Rowntree, 1901). His investigations identified two groups of people said to be in poverty – those in primary and those in secondary poverty. Primary poverty was defined as a state in which earnings were insufficient to maintain basic physical sufficiency. Secondary poverty was described as a state in which earnings were sufficient for physical efficiency but were spent inefficiently on unnecessary items. This has led some writers, such as John Veit-Wilson (1986), to argue that the concept of secondary poverty, although underpinned by notions of blame, that is, people in secondary poverty were spending their money improvidently, implied that a subjective account had been taken of those people's spending. This suggests that some consideration of the social context of poverty had to be accounted for. As Dean (2010) has identified, when Rowntree (1941) undertook a further study in determining what was considered the bare minimum of necessities, he expressly included items that were not present in his first study, such as a newspaper and tobacco. This means that even those more absolute approaches are not immune from current social influences such as changing social customs, cultural expectations and practices. As such they appeared to slip into Rowntree's list of items without much recognition or comment from himself.

Similar problems confront social workers on a daily basis in their interaction with service users living in poverty. Whether consciously or unconsciously, they will have some operational definition of poverty and will inevitably be assessing the levels of social and material resources available to that person or family, which in turn will influence how they respond to the needs presented. Gupta and Blewett (2008), in detailing service users' experiences of intervention by social workers, outlined how social workers approached the issue of poverty. Responses to service users included:

- ignoring the material poverty of service users, seeing this as the norm and therefore failing to recognise the impact on individuals and families;
- evidencing a prejudicial response in which service users were subject to moral opprobrium;
- looking at poverty as a risk factor in which families were judged as requiring child protection intervention rather than alleviating the risk factors associated with poverty.

Social workers who hold these assumptions will leave service users to exist at best at their current level of material poverty, with few opportunities to engage in wider cultural and social life. Wilton (2003) confirms this view in relation to service users in the field of mental health. His research showed the difficulties faced by poor service users that prevented them from participating in meaningful activities and opportunities to sustain social relationships. The notion of mere existence is therefore particularly dehumanising, as service users themselves testify:

> 'That's what distinguishes human beings from an animal. For the animal all it needs possibly is sufficient to live, where humans need something else and they are being denied that.' (Group of older people) (quoted in Beresford et al, 1999, p 53)

Encouraging AOP requires social workers to operate in a way that does not stigmatise and discriminate against service users who are poor. This entails a secure grounding in how poverty is defined, how it is measured and how people may end up living in poverty. When social workers interact with service users, how they conceptualise these different dimensions of poverty will inform their practice. For example, a social worker using an absolute definition of poverty in their practice will therefore assess service users only in terms of basic sufficiency rather than assessing a person's need for engaging in necessary and valued social practices, such as buying a Christmas present for a child or enabling a person to visit their elderly relatives in order to maintain their family network.

Measuring poverty

Social workers should be aware of how different approaches measure the extent of poverty in the UK. This is necessary because social workers need a general understanding of the extent of poverty, for example, in the particular areas and neighbourhoods in which they work, and also in relation to their individual work with service users. To understand the reality of living in poverty requires social workers to understand the particular way in which poverty is constituted for individuals and families. As Beresford et al (1999) argue, many service users do not always realise that they are living in poverty. Living at the economic margins of society can mean that service users become accustomed to living in ways that enable them to get by, and by so doing see their particular situation as the norm and not necessarily something that they would consider problematic. Therefore, to have a measure of poverty enables social workers to distinguish those living in relative poverty from those who are relatively well off. Social workers can therefore assess the consequences of poverty by measuring what is absent in terms of social opportunities and material living conditions.

Different approaches to measurement

Measuring poverty is usually approached by establishing an income threshold to ascertain how many individuals, families and households fall below it. This can be problematic in that a range of different and sometimes conflicting methods have been used. These methods vary by country and over time so that it becomes difficult to determine the most reliable method. Indeed, much controversy is involved where some, such as the present Coalition government (DWP, 2012a), question whether income by itself is a reliable indicator of poverty as against those (CAB, 2013) who would see income as a cornerstone in any measurement. Relative definitions take account of a range of indicators such as access to services or quality of social networks, which may be difficult to assess in relation to income. Nevertheless it is important to consider some of the more common approaches used to understand the nuances and challenges of poverty measurement.

Households living below sixty per cent of median income (after housing costs)

Successive governments in the UK have adopted the approach that households live in poverty if they have below 60 per cent of median income. Figures based on this calculation appear in the Households Below Average Income (HBAI) series (DWP 2003), and it is often given emphasis in the media; however, the DWP stresses that no single measure can accurately encapsulate the problem, so a number of other thresholds are also used (see Townsend, 2004). The problem with using such a measure is its arbitrary nature. Why is 60 per cent an adequate measure as opposed to 50 per cent, for example? Likewise, why is a median income used rather than a mean? Many feminist writers (for example, Lister, 2004) question the assumption that income is allocated fairly within households, so how do we account for who gets what within different households?

Social assistance benefit rates

Using actual assistance rates paid by the government to people on benefit has also been used as a measure. This would be a reasonable measure as long as we assume that the benefit levels paid are sufficient to take a person out of poverty. Unfortunately, this is not the case. For example, benefit levels rarely keep pace with the level of inflation or the level of wage rises in the economy. The Coalition government's social security policy introduced four major changes from April 2013. Three of these changes mean that affected claimants will experience cuts in their benefit in absolute terms:

- the 'bedroom tax' affecting housing benefit claimants in social housing deemed to have spare bedrooms;
- the replacement of council tax benefit by localised council tax support schemes;
- and the overall annual benefit cap on households.

The fourth change involves benefit cuts in real terms, i.e. the below-inflation uprating of out-of-work benefits and some elements of tax credits.

Overall 440,000 families are affected by these multiple benefit cuts, resulting in a loss of £16.90 a week for each of the families concerned (Aldridge and Tinson 2013). Many studies have shown the difference between actual benefit levels and what would be required in order for a person to be taken out of poverty. Townsend's study (1979) was perhaps one of the first to calculate that in order to take a person out of relative poverty, an increase of 40 per cent in benefit levels would need to be achieved. This is a sobering thought for social workers who, as mentioned earlier, work to a greater extent with people reliant on state benefits and therefore by definition those people will be living in significant poverty. As Townsend (2004) points out, benefit rates are not based on a consideration of minimum needs:

In fact the last time such an exercise was conducted officially was by Seebohm Rowntree in 1938. The National Assistance rates set in 1948 were based (loosely) on Rowntree's figures and it is not clear, given subsequent uprating policies and changes to benefit structures, what if any rationale exists for benefit levels today. (Townsend, 2004, p 14)

Budget standard

This approach seeks to collate a list of necessities, the absence of which can be used as a poverty line. This idea typically collects a weekly basket of goods that reflect the existing social needs of the time and that is then given a monetary value based on the costs of such goods. This may, on the surface, appear a useful way to determine existing poverty levels, but it does not get round the problem of arbitrary judgement, that is, who is making that judgement. It relies on the researcher/expert to determine what is considered a necessity to be included in the basket of goods, and does not account for the lived experience of people having to survive on those items deemed necessary by the expert.

The person most associated with this approach in the UK is Jonathan Bradshaw (1993) who has sought to construct a basket of goods that reflect what he considers to be a:

- low-cost but acceptable budget
- modest but adequate budget.

This work was based on complex calculations of people's expenditure and consumption of goods, and could be used to get a sense of what different types of family would be able to exist on in the two different types of budget.

Index of deprivation

This approach was originally developed by Townsend (1979) who hoped to move beyond the arbitrariness of previous research on poverty by surveying 2,000 households and asking them to reply as to whether they lacked (or not) items from a list of 60 indicators. As Alcock (2006) describes, around 40 of the indicators expressed as yes/no questions were significantly correlated with income. From these 40, Townsend identified 12 indicators, all of which correlated with a lack of income, and from this, a deprivation index was calculated for different households and compared with the incomes of households. After a complex calculation Townsend claimed that he had derived a deprivation threshold, a point at which income fell and deprivation increased disproportionately. This threshold was at about 140 per cent of Supplementary Benefit (currently Income Support) level. What differs in Townsend's approach is a consideration not just of budget standards but a broader conception of need, including, for example, housing, lifestyle, employment and access to services.

Exercise

Here is a list of Townsend's 12 indicators:

1) A week's holiday away from home
2) For adults, having a friend or relative to their home to eat in the last four weeks
3) For adults, going out or visiting a friend or relative in the last four weeks
4) For children, having a friend to play in the last four weeks
5) For children, not having a party on their last birthday
6) Not going out for entertainment in the last two weeks
7) Not having fresh meat at least four times a week
8) Not having a cooked meal one day in a fortnight
9) Not having a cooked breakfast most days of the week
10) Not having a house with a refrigerator
11) Where the household does not usually have a Sunday joint
12) Where the household lacks the sole use of four key amenities: flush w/c, sink/washbasin, fixed bath/shower, gas/electric cooker.

Accepting that this list was constructed 40 years ago, what strikes you about items related to the consumption of food in relation to your understanding today?

Reflection

I would guess that you may question the inclusion of item (9), for example, in the sense that lifestyles and eating habits have changed so much. Is it reasonable to equate not having a cooked breakfast most days of the week as an indicator of poverty? Likewise item (11) may reflect certain cultural assumptions regarding the importance of a Sunday joint. Would people from different cultures adhere to this practice? With the increase in the number of people who are vegetarian, does this account for their preferences? The preponderance of fast food outlets has also contributed to changes in people's eating habits, should recognition be afforded to these changes?

This example highlights the problems of researchers defining what they consider to be important indicators of poverty and then asking respondents their reaction to them.

The final approach that we consider attempts to get around such problems.

Refined deprivation indicator approach

This approach built on Townsend's study and attempted to overcome some of the problems outlined in the deprivation index approach. This analysis included choice in the calculation so that respondents were asked to identify a lack of necessities that were forced on them by presenting a list of items, and then asking the following:

1. To distinguish items they thought were necessary in the UK today (that is, that all adults should be able to afford and not have to go without) and those that were not.
2. To list the same items into three groups:
   a. Those they had
   b. Those they did not have but did not want
   c. Those they did not have and could not afford.

These items were placed into the list of necessities if over 50 per cent of people deemed them necessities. In total there were 35 items in this basket, ranging from beds and bedding, a refrigerator, two meals a day, an outfit for social occasions and a holiday away from home once a year. Deprivation scores were ranked against income to produce a poverty threshold. As a result, the authors defined 'poverty' as lacking two or more items.

This approach is attractive because the public themselves choose what they consider to be necessities. Nevertheless, the researcher still has to select the original list of items and activities presented to them. A further problem is that items are accepted as 'necessities' on a majority view even though particular items included in the list are not in fact considered necessities by a significant proportion of the population. Lastly, the perennial issue remains of how to account for changing needs that can be accommodated in the list of indicators.

Theories of poverty

> Is it the pig that makes the stye or the stye that makes the pig? That is – is the dirt and drinking habits of the lower class the cause or consequence of living in overcrowded buildings? (Royal Commission on Working Class Housing, 1884-1885). (Brown, 1973)

> For too long we have measured our success in tackling poverty in terms of the simplistic concept of income transfer. This strategy sets out a much more ambitious approach, aspiring to deliver Social Justice through life change which goes much wider than increases in family income alone. Social Justice must be about changing and improving lives, and the different ways this can be achieved. (DWP, 2012b, foreword by Iain Duncan-Smith)

The first quotation above reveals discriminatory attitudes towards people living in poverty; the second quotation, although using more measured words, nonetheless occupies the same style of reasoning as the Coalition government seeks to blame people who experience poverty for their own circumstances by calling for a change in their behaviour. The second quotation is wrapped up within the idea of social justice but nevertheless focuses more on changing the lives of the poor rather than the circumstances within which they live. Theories regarding the causes of poverty have been a contested area, and although recent governments of every political hue have begun to reflect an uneasy consensus on blaming the poor, this is not and has not always been the case. There are a conflicting range of explanations that this section outlines ranging from the individual to the structural in considering the causes of poverty. Explanations therefore vary, identifying:

- poor people being the authors of their own poverty;
- the values and beliefs reflected in cultural practices of people who experience poverty causing poverty;
- the nature of the environment in which people living in poverty live, which explains their poverty;
- the broader social relations in society underpinned by an unjust social economic system.

Examples of these different theories are now explored.

Poor people as authors of their own poverty

These theories of poverty contain within them a strong moral element based upon the reification of individualism and the notion of negative freedom. Within these approaches, therefore, people who experience poverty are considered lazy or morally bankrupt in the sense of not subscribing to what are considered majority views regarding the value of paid work and moral rectitude in relation to family life. Thus the objects for concern focus on individuals and family households who have never worked, individuals and families who repeatedly come into conflict with the moral authority of the state. This would involve, for example, committing crime, habitual substance misuse or flouting the assumed moral code of society by, for example, bringing up children (usually seen as teenage single mothers) without the presence of a father. One of the key words used here is dependence, which is seen as specific to this group of people, and is usually meant in terms of dependence on social security benefits. A key author in this regard is Charles Murray who, in a range of books and pamphlets mostly written in the 1980s, focused on what he considered to be the 'irresponsible' behaviour of people living in poverty. An 'underclass', using his terminology, had been formed, remaining more or less permanently dependent on the state to survive and showing no willingness to improve their lot. The extent of this moral discourse was encapsulated in a pamphlet Murray (1994) wrote calling the underclass the 'new rabble'. Successive governments have either consciously adopted this approach in developing more punitive approaches to those claiming social security benefits, particularly those considered 'the able-bodied poor', or focusing on particular groups of people considered to exhibit long-standing dependency and troubled behaviour. This can be seen more recently in relation to social work in the focus on 'problem families'. Prime Minister David Cameron outlined the present Coalition government's position:

> Officialdom might call them "families with multiple disadvantages". Some in the press might call them "neighbours from hell". Whatever you call them, we've known for years that a relatively small number of families are the source of a large proportion of the problems in society. Drug addiction. Alcohol abuse. Crime. A culture of disruption and irresponsibility that cascades through generations…. Last year the state spent an estimated £9 billion on just 120,000 families…. (Cameron, 2011)

This focus on the behaviour of the poorest in society echoes those attitudes redolent of the Victorian Poor Law, distinguishing an undeserving minority from the majority of 'hard working families', a phrase often used by politicians today to demonise people who live in poverty. Individualistic explanations often focus on poverty being a rational choice made by those who prefer to live on social security where it is argued they receive a higher income than if they were in work. A rational choice balances costs against benefits, and where the individual assesses that a particular action is beneficial in terms of this calculus, they will choose accordingly. This assumption takes little account of how a person's motivation is constructed socially and psychologically; nor does it recognise that people may make decisions that do not fit with maximising their benefits over the costs accrued. Many service users may not have the knowledge or capability to make a rational choice; others may be living in situations that impede their ability to make a rational choice yet still remain living in poverty. Others, such as asylum seekers, see any capability to 'choose' to come off benefits removed by legislation surrounding asylum which prevents them from working. Recent research from the US has documented the difficulties that people living in poverty have in making rational choices. Mullainathan and Shafir (2013) argue that poverty has deleterious effects on the mind which lead poor people to make impoverished choices. Living in poverty imposes significant psychological costs that reduces our capacity to make decisions that could alleviate such a condition.

Poverty as culture

Social workers may work with families who have a long history of involvement with social services. It is tempting to suggest that these families reinforce their poverty by their attitudes towards, for example, what are considered to be acceptable moral norms of work. The explanation that poverty is a function of poorly formed attitudes towards key moral norms is not new. In the 1970s a Conservative politician, Keith Joseph, propagated the theory of a 'cycle of deprivation'. For

Joseph there was a generational process at work whereby the values and attitudes of one generation were passed onto the next through inadequate socialisation. Unacceptable and deviant norms and values were dysfunctional in socialising children to improve their position in society. This may not be a culture that was necessarily oppositional to the majority, but was often characterised by a lack of agency on behalf of people living in poverty who adopted fatalistic ideas about moving out of poverty and settled for accepting their lot and 'getting by'. This was apparently supported by work from the US by Lewis (1968), who observed of Puerto Rican families how they had learned to cope with high levels of poverty. Coping mechanisms included a lack of ambition for themselves or their children, which accommodated their poor status. Families adopted ingenious ways of coping on a meagre income which enabled them to survive from one day to the next. These ideas were tested in the UK by Rutter and Madge (1976); although preferring to use the term 'disadvantage' rather than 'deprivation', they found little evidence to suggest a strong association of generational influence in determining the life chances of children. As the study extended its reach from two generations of families to three, the evidence became even slimmer. They were able to conclude:

> On the one hand, even where continuity is strongest many individuals break out of the cycle and on the other many people become disadvantaged without having been reared by disadvantaged parents. (Rutter and Madge, 1976, p 52)

Recent work by Macmillan (2011), using the example of worklessness across generations, found only 15,000 households in the UK that have two or more generations who report having 'never worked' or who have two or more generations with significant time out of work; this amounts to 0.8 per cent of all households in the UK.

Macmillan (2011) goes on to show that local labour market conditions are crucial in determining any generational effect. In labour markets where unemployment is high, sons with workless fathers in childhood spend on average 25–30 per cent more time out of work than sons with employed fathers in childhood in the same local labour market. By contrast, in tight labour markets, where unemployment is low, there is no difference in the labour market experience of sons, whether their fathers were workless or employed during the sons' childhoods. This means that any intergenerational link is a factor of the labour market rather than the transmission of a poor work ethic.

As Harkness et al (2012) argue, the Coalition government's policy to reduce levels of benefit in order to 'incentivise' the unemployed in areas with high levels of unemployment will have serious consequences. The result may be:

> ... that multiple deprivation in these areas with few jobs would lead marginal workers (those with the weakest attachment to the labour

market) to suffer most in weak labour markets and become even worse off. (Harkness et al, 2012, p 20)

Finally, a study that set out specifically to investigate the notion of intergenerational worklessness concluded:

> We believe this to be the first study to have interrogated, explicitly, the idea that there are families where "three generations have never worked". The notion of intergenerational cultures of worklessness might be a captivating and convenient means of trying to explain patterns of worklessness but the evidence collected in this research project, from families most likely to fit the thesis, leads us to conclude that the phenomenon is more imagined than real. (Shildrick et al, 2012, p 47)

Poverty and the social environment

As the 19th century drew to a close, different explanations for the causes of poverty competed with the previously dominant individual accounts. The failure of the social environment began to be identified as a significant explanation of poverty. As argued, the Royal Commission on the Poor Laws in 1908 had as one of its starting points to investigate the ways in which people who experience poverty may not necessarily be responsible for their fate. Some of the key issues at this time were unemployment, casual and irregular low wage employment. This was exemplified in the East End of London by the way dock workers were hired on a casual basis, therefore having no security of employment. The operation of national and local labour markets was crucial in determining levels of employment; even when wage levels were adequate (which was rare), the level of poverty of those in work remained high. These issues remain today with an increasing casualisation of the workforce, some 300,000 care workers are employed on zero hours contracts where employees can be called upon at a moment's notice to work. This leaves workers with little idea what hours they will be working in the week and potentially causing significant financial difficulties (TUC, 2013). The unemployment rate in the UK was last reported at 8.2 per cent from February to May of 2012. Historically, from 1971 until 2012, the unemployment rate in the UK averaged 7.2 per cent, reaching an all time high of 12.0 per cent in February of 1984 and a record low of 3.4 per cent in November of 1973. These variations in the unemployment rate therefore have little to do with an individual's willingness to work, and more to do with the operation of the global economy. At times of economic crisis it can often be wider economic conditions and a government's response that can determine levels of unemployment and poverty. The current economic crisis has seen the Coalition government seeking to retrench the economy in the light of the banking crisis and the downturn in exports to the global market. Current responses to the economic crisis are a case in point;

comparing unemployment rates within the European Community highlight this further. For example, in January 2010 unemployment in Greece was 11.75 per cent; by January 2012, it was 22.65 per cent as a result of government policies in cutting back public services, reducing pensions and benefits and raising taxes.

There are other characteristics in the social environment that may also lead to the poverty of people that are related to issues of discrimination. For example, the Disability Movement in the UK has long campaigned for equality of access for people with disabilities into the educational system and following on, into the labour market. The social exclusion of people with disabilities from the mainstream of society has therefore led to significant levels of poverty among this group. Disablist attitudes are often reflected in the way in which the social environment is structured towards the needs of the able-bodied. The impact of disability on income is therefore profound:

- Disabled adults are twice as likely to live in low-income households as non-disabled adults, and this has been the case throughout the last decade.
- Disabled adults in workless families are actually somewhat less likely to be in low income than their non-disabled counterparts.
- For all family types, a disabled adult's risk of being in low income is much greater than that for a non-disabled adult. (The Poverty Site, 2013)

In identifying the social environment as problematic for groups of people devalued by society, we are focusing not on the attitudes of those so defined negatively, such as 'the poor' or benefit claimants or people with disabilities, but on the attitudes in society towards those groups. These attitudes are therefore significant factors in generating poverty for socially stigmatised groups such as people with disabilities. A writer not often used in the context of poverty is Wolfensberger (1992). His work in relation to people with learning disabilities highlighted the ways in which society both negatively valued people with learning disabilities and also reinforced this within the institutions of society, leading to their marginalisation. The exclusion of people with disabilities within mainstream social institutions left people with learning disabilities with few opportunities for participation in society at large. These issues can be evaluated across a range of groups within society who may be systematically discriminated against in terms of, for example, class, 'race' or gender.

Structural explanations of poverty

Structural explanations for the existence of poverty explore the way existing social relations in society result in persistent inequalities in wealth and income. The focus on inequality looks at the barriers to those at the bottom of the income pyramid to move out of poverty and the wealth of opportunities and advantages accruing to those at the top. Marxist approaches add a further dimension in examining the nature of the capitalist economic and social system which is identified as the problem in reinforcing economic and social inequality. This is achieved by powerful groups and individuals (the capitalist class) controlling this system for their benefit to the detriment of the majority (the working class). It is the role of the state which is tied to and operates in the interests of the dominant capitalist class to administer this system on behalf of the capitalist. Thus policies such as those related to social security to alleviate poverty will always be piecemeal in this view and will not radically alter the condition of people living in poverty. Indeed, Marxists argue that poverty has a central role in disciplining the population to ensure that inactivity and idleness is punished and hard work rewarded, however meagre this may be for some (Ferguson et al, 2002).

For some writers (for example, Alcock, 2006), the Marxist analysis has its dangers as it becomes little more than stating the obvious by identifying the problem without being able to identify the means to alleviate poverty. Clearly for Marxist writers this will only be achieved by an overthrow of the capitalist system; this does not, in Alcock's view, provide a realistic prognosis for policy action. On the one hand, there is much to commend this viewpoint from a reformist position. Different societies have different policy responses to the problem of poverty, which leads to greater or lesser hardship for poor people and varying levels of poverty, as any study of different welfare states policies towards poverty would reveal. But there are other viewpoints that can qualify Alcock's argument. For example, in outlining the different explanations of poverty, these are not benign and influence the policy towards people living in poverty by recent governments. The way in which poverty is understood, for example, by representations of poverty through the media, may also be reflected in the attitudes of the population at large, as the British Social Attitudes (Park et al, 2012) survey suggests. Some Marxist writers have taken a more nuanced view of policy development, and suggest, as Gough (1979, 2000) and Stiller and van Kersbergen (2005) have done, that advances in policy have been won by the working class and global social movements, and represent advances that have provided some minimum protection for working people. For social workers working with service users, being able to explain a service user's position as not being a consequence of deficient cultural attitudes or as a result of individual failure therefore requires an understanding of the structural reasons for poverty that may be obvious to some policymakers but not necessarily the wider population. This means that these ideas should be translated at the individual level as service users may blame themselves for their poverty and some social workers may in turn blame service users.

The extent to which policies can be developed which offer real improvements to people experiencing poverty remain as contested as the theories that seek to explain them. For social workers it is important to realise that differences in policy can and are achieved by human intervention at all levels. While theories inform practice, social workers will need to develop their own understanding of why people continue to live in poverty, and then act on them, both at an individual level with service users and within the wider community and society at large. If the profession of social work is to continue, then it needs to recognise that the social remains their object of concern in understanding and combating poverty. Theories that individualise the condition of the poor and that inevitably lead to the blaming and scapegoating of poor people will not provide the theoretical and explanatory tools necessary for social workers to work effectively to eradicate poverty.

Summary

This chapter has explained the importance of conceptualising poverty for social workers. It has highlighted that how social workers define poverty will influence the way that they will then work with service users. It has identified the importance of understanding how poverty can be measured so that social workers can use this knowledge to determine the extent of poverty within the lives of service users and the communities in which they live. Finally, it has explored the different theories employed to understand why people may become poor and how they remain living in poverty. The importance in adopting social structural explanations has been argued for in order to avoid stigmatising and blaming those people living in poverty for their own fate and in order to adopt more effective policies to eliminate poverty.

Recommended reading

Alcock, P. (2006) *Understanding poverty*, Basingstoke: Palgrave.
Dean, H. (2010) *Understanding human need*, Bristol: Policy Press.

3

The reform of welfare?

The government faces many social and economic challenges in trying to alleviate poverty. On the one hand, with relatively short-term demographic changes, for example, as society ages, policy will reflect higher spending on pensions and an increased demand for health and social care services. On the other hand, in a global economy, many governments are seeking to limit their social costs in order to attract global corporations to invest in their countries, while also grappling with the aftershock of the banking crisis which has seen state financial support to the banking sector amount to £850 billion of guarantees and loans (National Audit Office, 2011). Both the Coalition government and the Labour Party in opposition agree on the importance of meeting these challenges in terms of cutting public spending; the difference is one of degree in terms of the rate at which public spending should be cut, and how far the government should intervene to maintain levels of employment while this process is undertaken. Meeting the challenges of an ageing population and maintaining suitable levels of public services must be set against the Coalition government's policy of austerity to maintain the downward trajectory of public spending. Austerity is likely to shape the context of policy responses and to have an impact on levels of intervention to tackle poverty in the future (see Taylor-Gooby, 2011).

Social security policy directed at people living in poverty has historically been concerned with how the efficiency of the economy can be maintained while trying to maintain the work ethic of people who experience poverty (Grover, 2010). In Chapter 1 we identified these concerns as they were expressed in the 19th century through the Poor Law reforms. Recent governments of different political persuasions have also concerned themselves with these questions and have shown a certain level of consensus on what should be 'done' with those living in poverty. Governments have sought to balance what they consider to be the proper role of government to support poor people with the responsibilities that they argue those who experience poverty have for themselves. This responsibility agenda involves not just the able-bodied poor in terms of work, but also includes, for example, people with disabilities being more work-focused, and families, in particular single-parent families, becoming more work-ready by undertaking suitable education and training.

The focus on responsibility is therefore a recurring feature of all governments over the past 20 years. As Griggs and Bennett (2009) argue, when the Labour government came to office in 1997, the idea of a contract between claimants and the state took on an increasing significance whereby help to people living in poverty was increasingly tied in with their responsibility to find work if they could. Conditions were placed on 'jobseekers' to increase their efforts to find work while receiving benefits and also being required to offer themselves for training and education. Likewise, Labour continued the trend of reducing non-contributory benefits with an increase in means-tested benefits. These trends were also evident across Europe and represented a focus on activation (getting people into work through placing conditions on benefit entitlement) and in some cases, workfare (working in return for benefit).

The focus on work is argued as the best route out of poverty and has figured within the Coalition government's policies. This assumption, that work is the best route out of poverty, requires investigation. For example, if social workers are to advise service users as to how they can move out of poverty, then recourse to the evidence is required. But before considering the evidence, I suggest you read the following case study.

Case study: Jill and Robert

You are working with a young family; both partners, Jill and Robert, are 22 years old, and they have two children, a boy (Levi) and a girl (Jaden), aged 1 and 2 respectively. Both adults have been out of out of work for nine months and they are beginning to incur some debt, particularly in relation to their energy bills, where they are having to take money they should be spending on food in order to meet their arrears. There is a chance that some permanent work will become available for Jill as she saw a vacancy advertised at the job centre. The level of pay is not good, but when Jill talked to the job adviser, he calculated that they would be receiving £10 a week more with the new universal Working Tax Credit than they would receive on benefit. Jill is eager to apply for the job while Robert is not sure; they ask you for any advice that you can give.

What kind of issues would you suggest Jill and Robert consider in helping them make a decision?

Reflection

I am sure that you have found this difficult if you do not know some of the evidence considered below. Nevertheless, you may have felt that the extra money is positive, as is the idea of the experience of work for Jill after a relatively long time unemployed. So you will probably encourage the family to make a decision to accept the offer of work. However, your advice may need to be tempered a little.

First, how successful is this policy in getting people into work, irrespective at this stage of whether it lifts people out of poverty? Daguerre and Etherington (2009), in a research paper for the Department for Work and Pensions (DWP), reported that activation reforms have had mixed results. They remark that some programmes only had a positive impact (although they are not clear what this means) after two or three years, while more workfare-oriented benefit sanctions, with increased work requirements, while cost-effective in the short term in decreasing those claiming benefit, was relatively short-lived. As they observe:

> ... such programmes do not always foster sustainable employment as participants tend to cycle back and forth between low paid jobs and benefits. (Daguerre and Etherington, 2009, p 21)

More tellingly, they argue that as the economic recession progresses and certain jobs disappear, then:

> ... the effectiveness of the deterrence or motivation effects might reach its limits, simply because people will have to get back on benefits. (p 21)

The impact of these various activation schemes has also been investigated in Europe, and similar conclusions have been drawn. Eichhorst and Konle-Seidl (2008) compared activation programmes across Europe and found that there were short-term benefits from the compulsory elements of the programmes. However, it is likely, as some evidence suggests, that the more coercive programmes may scare benefit recipients into low-skill, low-paid and less stable jobs, which run the risk of continued or partial reliance on a return to benefits. They conclude:

> There is no clear evidence that activation as such necessarily leads to lower overall benefit dependency and public expenditure. Activation, therefore, is neither cheap nor easy – and it may not be the silver bullet to ease fiscal pressures on the welfare state by increasing overall employment and reducing benefit expenditure. (Eichhorst and Konle-Seidl, 2008, p 24)

The government's own Social Security Advisory Committee (SSAC, 2012) reviewed the literature on the application of sanctions and found some difficulties in operating such systems. In particular, the most disadvantaged and vulnerable claimants experience sanctions more disproportionately than others, in particular those most socially deprived and those on longer-term benefits. Claimants with low self-esteem and low skills were also at higher risk of receiving sanctions. In general, those claimants who may be identified as non-compliant with the various sanction regimes do not do so deliberately, but have poor organisational skills. They may experience other problems such as mental health problems or mild learning disabilities, and as a consequence have difficulty in understanding the sanctions imposed and may forget the conditions they are supposed to fulfil. This means that social workers have to be mindful of this regime for the service users they work with as service users may be unfairly targeted with sanctions. Job Centre Plus staff will also require a greater degree of training in using their professional discretion to be aware of the additional problems (such as mental health issues) claimants may face. Given that the evidence in favour of activation is at best thin, how effective are these arrangements in taking people out of poverty?

The Joseph Rowntree Trust sponsored a review of research (Goulden, 2010) that looked at four research projects:

- two were based on interviews with single people and families with children in or at the margins of insecure labour markets;
- one looked at the perspectives of employers;
- one investigated recurrent poverty from the longitudinal British Household Panel Survey (BHPS).

Goulden (2010) noted that research from national survey data showed a strong association between *persistent* poverty and poor people experiencing multiple transitions in and out of work (see also Adelman et al, 2003). The consequence of this 'recycling' means that certain kinds of employment (insecure, low-paid work with poor working conditions) could in some cases mean individuals and families are worse off than if they had not been in employment at all. This is so because of the inflexibility of the benefits system, in which those moving in and out of work have to face a round of continual assessment and reassessment for their benefits once they are out of work. Paradoxically, the requirements placed on jobseekers to be flexible, by moving in and out of benefit to access work, is not matched by the flexibility of the benefits system when this process is reversed.

Goulden's summary showed how the conditions of someone's employment could affect their chances of getting trapped in a cycle of poverty – employment per se is not a panacea. The summary confirms that employment remains the best defence against poverty, but employment that provides:

- a permanent contract
- chance of promotion
- a chance of a pay rise
- associated in-work benefits, for example, a company pension.

Although individual characteristics may play a role in maintaining a person in recurrent poverty, structural factors in the wider global economy and the national labour market have by far the strongest impact. Thus, in order to combat poverty, certain factors need to be in place if social workers are to advise service users with confidence that work will necessarily lead to better outcomes for them. These factors include:

- improving rights and conditions for low-paid and agency workers;
- increasing pay through 'living wage' campaigns;
- ensuring that the benefits system is flexible and responsive.

Exercise

Having looked at some of the evidence in relation to the benefits of encouraging people into work and the assumption that work lifts people out of poverty, what would your advice to Jill and Robert be now?

Reflection

There is a clear tension here between the promises of some short-term financial gains for the family against some of the attendant risks outlined earlier. Although it is not clear how long the job may last, nor is it clear whether it will lead to a permanent contract, would this family be put into a position of having to reapply for benefit with all the attendant problems this entails when the job finishes, such as:

- Making a new claim for Jobseeker's Allowance?
- The complexity of the application process and subsequent interview at the job centre?
- Possible delay in receiving benefit?
- The gap between the last pay day in work and receiving benefit?
- The danger of moving further into debt as a result of the above?

On accepting employment the family could lose other benefits that they are entitled to, such as free school meals (FSM) and free prescriptions, which will depend on their overall income. These calculations are usually done by the job adviser at the job centre. Nevertheless, Jill and Robert would need to understand these issues before seeing their adviser. In the event of refusing to take up the job, Jill could face having her benefit withdrawn if it is interpreted that she refused for illegitimate reasons.

One final point in respect to the government's attempts to activate people into work has emerged in the findings of the House of Commons Public Accounts Committee (2013). This Committee monitors government spending, and investigated the effectiveness of the government's Work Programme whereby private agencies are contracted to help claimants to find work. They found the Programme was failing – from June 2011 to July 2012, only 3.6 per cent of people referred to the Work Programme moved off benefit and into sustained employment, which is less than a third of the level expected. None of the 18 private agencies met their minimum performance targets. Equally damning was the realisation that the actual performance was below the Department's (DWP) assessment of the non-intervention rate, that is, the number of people who would have found sustained work had the Work Programme not been running at all.

The issue of work and poverty is therefore a highly complex one, and social workers who may feel that work irrespective of any other calculation is necessarily a good thing may need to re-evaluate this understanding in the light of the evidence presented here.

Welfare Reform Act 2012

We now turn to look at the main changes to social security introduced by the Coalition government. The Welfare Reform Act received its royal assent in March 2012. One of its main provisions is to introduce a Universal Credit, to replace:

• Housing Benefit
• Income Support
• income-related Employment and Support Allowance
• income-based Jobseeker's Allowance
• Working Tax Credit and Child Tax Credit.

Universal Credit is to be welcomed for its apparent simplicity in replacing an array of benefits with one overarching payment, yet problems remain. Many organisations representing different groups affected by these changes have provided some useful critiques which will be drawn on in this section. These groups act as advocates for poor people and those with a range of other needs such as mental health service users, people with disabilities and so on.

The rationale for Universal Credit is to address the barriers that service users face moving from benefit into employment and vice versa. The intention is to ensure claimants will be able to take up any amount of work without the disruption of losing Income Support as their claim for one benefit shuts down and a new one begins. With the benefit of improved IT systems, Universal Credit will be calculated using real-time information about wages, rather than the lagged data on which tax credits have been based. As a result, incomes should not face the disruption currently experienced, and budgeting on these incomes should be made easier (CPAG, 2012).

Universal Credit also features a strong element of control, particularly in relation to couples. Payment of the benefit will be assessed jointly, so if one partner is penalised for failure to abide by the conditions of payment of benefit, then the other partner will be affected too. Other more oppressive elements of this benefit include the following:

• in claiming Universal Credit claimants will be required to work more hours or seek a more highly paid job in order to reach the income threshold for when payment starts;
• claimants will be expected to look for work further away from home than at present (with a 90-minute as opposed to the current 60-minute commute being considered reasonable under the new regime);
• claimants will be expected to seek work sooner if they have children from the age of five rather than seven, as it currently stands.

Many groups representing claimants have been particularly critical of Universal Credit being paid on a monthly rather than a fortnightly basis. For example, as we shall see below, service users are already reporting difficulties in making ends meet from one fortnight to the next; the additional time lapse and the potential pressure to pay off debt may leave individuals and families struggling even more. Social workers working with people who already have difficulty in budgeting, due, for example, to a learning disability or a mental health problem, will therefore need to be more aware of the pressures placed on service users in budgeting over a longer time frame than they may be used to.

Paradoxically, Universal Credit, with its avowed intention of incentivising people to take up paid work, has some regressive elements in this regard. Both the Child Poverty Action Group (CPAG, 2012) and Save the Children (2012a) highlight the weakness of incentives to lone parents and second earners within a family. Help with childcare costs will be less than that provided under tax credits before April 2011, further hindering some claimants from taking up work. Likewise, families with disabled children will lose out on critical support. Currently, parents of disabled children who receive Disability Living Allowance get a 'disability element' top-up to their Child Tax Credit of £53.62 per week for each disabled child. This money is used to pay for the additional costs involved in bringing up a disabled child, such as wear and tear to clothes and equipment. Within Universal Credit, the equivalent 'disability addition' will fall to £26.75 per week (Mencap, 2012).

The overall distribution of income within families is also likely to be affected. Under the current system, Child Tax Credit is paid to the main carer (usually by default in heterosexual couples the woman); under Universal Credit, payment will be made to the main earner (usually the man). Previously the principle informing payment was to ensure that the person who had main responsibility for providing for the children received the benefit; an element of control over the family income is now removed for the main carer, which may mean less income being available for children in the family.

In Chapter 1 we outlined some of the early provisions of the Poor Law (Amendment) Act 1834 and in particular focused on the principle of less eligibility. This principle stated that any relief given within the workhouse should be less than what the lowest paid labourer could expect in wages. The Coalition government has instituted a similar principle in the WRA 2012. In future a household's total benefit payment will be capped at average earnings, although households in receipt of Working Families Tax Credit, containing war widows or someone with a disability, will be exempted. This policy change was introduced in terms of fairness. As David Cameron observed:

> Take a couple living outside London. He's a hospital porter, she's a care-worker. They're both working full-time and together they take home £24,000 after tax. They'd love to start having children – and they know they'd get some help from the state if they did so. But with the mortgage and the bills to pay, they feel they should keep saving up for a few more years. But the couple down the road, who have four children, haven't worked for a number of years. Each week they get

£112 in Income Support, £61 in Child Benefit, £217 in tax credits and £141 in Housing Benefit – more than £27,000 a year. Even after the £26,000 benefit cap is introduced, they'll still take home more than their neighbours who go out to work every day. Can we really say that's fair? (quoted in *Daily Telegraph*, 2012a)

Taking Cameron's example at face value, the notion of fairness seems disingenuous. As we can see, we are not comparing like with like; if the couple in work had four children, then they would also be entitled to Child Tax Credit, and depending on the status of the children, that is, whether they were in full-time education or not, the amount of credit would vary. Using figures supplied by HMRC via their tax credit calculator, I worked out that for three children in full-time education and one child in a nursery, and using the income of a couple of £24,000 per year, the total tax credit available could be £9,105. This takes the couple's income above that of the unemployed couple. We might also comment that the amount that the unemployed couple is receiving includes Housing Benefit which is not disposable income; benefit to live on after rent is paid is a bare minimum. In addition we might question how fair it is for a working couple to be receiving, after tax, £24,000. Is this a problem of benefits being too generous or a problem of inadequate wages? Employers are only too willing to pay what they consider the market rate for the job, but this is not the same as paying a living wage, as mentioned earlier, hence the need for tax credits and also the need for minimum wage legislation. As Aldridge et al (2012) observe, 6.1 million people in poverty are in working households. If pensioners are excluded from these figures, in-work poverty now outstrips workless poverty, at 5.1 million households. In addition, the circulation of people moving into poverty or out of work is significant, with 18 per cent of people living on a low income at any one time, 33 per cent experiencing at least one period of low income in a four-year period, and 11 per cent in low income for more than half of that time.

In addition to the proposals we have already focused on within the WRA 2012, two other changes to social security payments have made a significant impact: first, Housing Benefit affecting people with large families living in inner-city privately rented accommodation, and second, people with disabilities.

Changes to Housing Benefit

Public spending on Housing Benefit increased from £11 billion in 1999/2000 to £22 billion in 2011. Housing Benefit is characterised as being poorly administered by local authorities, leaving claimants in vulnerable circumstances. An Audit Commission report (2012) identified that 75 per cent of local authorities take on average six weeks to process a new claim, with some claimants having to wait for six months or even longer. The National Association of Citizens' Advice Bureaux (NACAB) receives in the region of 70 reports a month concerning evictions being threatened due to delay in reaching decisions on Housing Benefit. Given its policies of deficit reduction and reducing public expenditure, the Coalition government has targeted this benefit as an area to make significant savings. In terms of the government's position, Housing Benefit, where it is paid particularly to larger families residing in higher rental areas in the inner cities (mainly in the South East of the UK and London), provides a disincentive to work. Claimants have to earn higher incomes in work in order to pay their rent, something which is particularly difficult given that those on benefit in general will be likely to access work in the lower wage bands. In terms of the government's own figures, this measure will save the Treasury £3 billion over a five-year period from 2012 (DWP, 2010). The government allows a maximum of £400 per week to be paid for a four-bedroomed property, which will become the maximum cap; additional caps will also cover properties with fewer bedrooms. In addition, the maximum Local Housing Allowance will be set at the 30th percentile rather than the median, that is, the 50th. This means that in London, for example, only three in ten properties in any broad rental market area are likely to be affordable to people on Housing Benefit (Fenton, 2010).

Service users on Housing Benefit will be given nine months from April 2011 before these measures take effect. The impact by restricting the four-bedroom rate will increase, in the government's words, 'the number of tenants facing shortfalls between their benefit and contractual rent, if current rent levels and accommodation choices did not change' (DWP, 2010, p 8).

The government argues that the purpose of reform is to influence rent levels and housing choices, which is likely, they argue, to mitigate the impact of these measures. The DWP (2010) estimates that of the 939,220 households on local authority caseloads, 936,960 will lose out, with the average loss calculated at £12 a week. In London, where the caseload is 159,370, all these households will lose on average £22 a week or be forced to move. Overall 50 per cent of households will lose on average £13 a week. It is interesting to note that the government prefers to target tenants paying high levels of rent rather than controlling the overall level of rents that private landlords can charge.

The 'Bedroom Tax'

Working-age claimants who are deemed to have a spare bedroom in their council or housing association home will be faced with a reduction in their Housing Benefit. Those affected claiming Housing Benefit have faced these reductions since 1 April 2013; the government hopes this will force tenants to move to a smaller property to free larger properties for families. The government's own Impact Assessment describes that affected households will lose between £13 and £14 a week, with some 40,000 households losing all their entitlement to Housing Benefit. In addition:

> If all existing social sector tenants wished to move to accommodation
> of an appropriate size, there would be a mismatch between available
> accommodation and the needs of tenants. (DWP, 2012c)

This policy has been 'designed' with the aim, so the government argues, of reducing waiting lists for social housing. The hope is that families on council waiting lists will then be able to move into property vacated by tenants who no longer need an extra bedroom. However, as the government's own Impact Assessment makes clear, if this policy is successful in forcing people to look for one- and two-bedroom properties, these properties are not available. These problems are further exacerbated where rent for properties is high or in rural areas, where the range of properties may not be available. This will mean significant stress and disruption for people on top of the further changes to Housing Benefit identified earlier. The Resolution Foundation(2013) has reported that in 125 of 376 local authorities in the UK couples with one child and a net income of £22,000 a year would have to spend more than 35 per cent of their income to rent the cheapest two-bedroom property, making it unaffordable to live there. In effect this policy has not been thought through; it targets poor families and expects them to shoulder the responsibility for the lack of affordable housing. This policy masks the inability of successive governments to build affordable homes to rent. Since the Housing Act 1980, which instituted a 'Right to Buy' policy for tenants in council houses, there has been a steady erosion in the numbers of available properties. Legislation prevented local authorities from using the proceeds of sales to build new homes. Thus waiting lists have steadily climbed for social housing, and there are now 1.8 million households on local authorities waiting lists.

Implications for social work

The DWP (2010) argues that families receiving social work support who may need to move face additional disruption. This could mean families losing contact with children and families social work departments, which is particularly worrying for those children deemed at greater risk. It also means that some social services departments may face increased workloads requiring additional resources, although where these resources may come from is unclear, as the government is not proposing any transitional arrangements in these cases. In relation to people with disabilities, there may be additional problems. For example, tenancies in the private rented sector are an increasing option for people with learning and other disabilities who are considered for independent living. Some of the properties will have required adaptations to be put in place, so requiring new adaptations if they have to move. Some discretionary payments may be available to enable people with disabilities to remain in their property if the cost of removal is deemed higher than the savings achieved. However, the loss of contact with informal carers and friends and the loss of social work support will require significant reassessments of the needs of people with disabilities to be made by the local authority where the person moves to. This will add a great deal of stress to the people with disabilities themselves and, of course, relatives and friends who may not be able to support the person so easily in their home if they move some distance away.

Overall, some 48 per cent of households affected will include children. Although families with four or more children account for less than 5 per cent of all families, they are disproportionately represented, at 20 per cent of all poor children. These families are therefore at higher risk of unemployment and also at higher risk of experiencing a wider range of social problems, and are more likely to have received social work services. Requiring these families to move and only receiving Housing Benefit for a four-bedroom property is likely to increase the risk of overcrowding as families move into properties with fewer bedrooms. This, in turn, will have adverse consequences for stress within families and poorer health outcomes. For children in such families disruption to schooling and loss of social networks is also likely to have an impact. Another group likely to be effected are those single-parent families, particularly families with teenage mothers, who are likely to lose the support of social work and other services such as Connexions as they are forced to move. This will have a further impact in terms of isolation and added stress, which is likely to affect their mental health (see Gould, 2006).

From Incapacity Benefit to Employment and Support Allowance

The Coalition government, like the previous Labour government, has been concerned that too many people on Incapacity Benefit are not actively encouraged to find work. The Labour government shifted Incapacity Benefit to Employment and Support Allowance, which was designed to move people with disabilities into being work-ready.

Employment and Support Allowance is the new out-of-work benefit for people with disabilities. Since 2008 new applicants for out-of-work disability benefits have been directed to Employment and Support Allowance. The shift towards this benefit focused on what people could do in terms of their capabilities, and not on what they could not do in terms of their disabilities. This has led one blogger (DavidG, 2012) to observe:

> Yet capability and incapacity may often be diametrically opposed. To use my own situation as an example, I am capable of work that many people might label "rocket science", yet doing that work results in rapidly rising pain levels, which in turn interferes severely with my ability to work at that level and ultimately prevents me from working at all. It is difficult to accomplish much while curled in a foetal position on the floor as a result of the levels of pain working has engendered. Any assessment which does not focus on both my capability and my incapacity will necessarily fail me.

While the focus on assessing a person's ability may be welcome although problematic for some like DavidG, many disability groups have long been supportive of enabling people with disabilities to access the labour market; nonetheless, this policy has a number of flaws. People's eligibility for Employment and Support Allowance is dependent on a Work Capability Assessment (WCA). This involves the applicant filling out a form about their disability and then attending a medical assessment. In the assessment, applicants score points based on various 'descriptors' relating to physical and mental health. Following this assessment a government 'decision maker' allocates the person to one of three groups:

* 'Fit for work', meaning they will be required to seek work and therefore receive Jobseeker's Allowance.
* 'Work-related Activity Group', which means they must involve themselves in activities which will help them prepare for work while still claiming Employment and Support Allowance.
* 'Support Group', meaning they are not required to seek or prepare for work and receive a higher rate of Employment and Support Allowance.

From 2010 until 2014 most people currently claiming one of the existing incapacity benefits will be transferred to the new Employment and Support Allowance; this will involve the majority of existing claimants of incapacity benefits being reassessed via the WCA.

In order to monitor the progress and effectiveness of the changes, the government instituted an independent review (Harrington, 2010, 2011). In the first review Harrington (2010) identified that the WCA was not fit for purpose and had attracted much criticism as to its fairness. In particular:

> There is strong evidence that the system can be impersonal and mechanistic, that the process lacks transparency and that a lack of communication between the various parties involved contributes to poor decision making and a high rate of appeals. (Harrington, 2010, p 8)

The review made recommendations for improving the assessment, which the government acquiesced to. Harrington also requested that Mind, Mencap and the National Autistic Society assess the test in regard to mental health and learning disabilities, and make further recommendations. Mind is particularly critical of the WCA and has argued that the process should be halted until the system is working more equitably (Mind, 2012). Evidence from the pilot projects set up to test the system is also negative. Roxborough (2011), a welfare rights manager in Burnley, identified a number of problems with the process that have subsequently been confirmed by such organisations as Mind above. First, the forms used to assess people for Employment and Support Allowance are more complex and time-consuming; this is the case for people with learning disabilities and with mental health problems. If a claimant migrates to Employment and Support Allowance and is placed in the Work-related Activity Group rather than the Support Group, they have to respond to a new set of requirements involving frequent work-focused interviews; again these can be intimidating for people not used to this kind of regime. The WCA is also stricter than the previous test under Incapacity Benefit. For example, inability to raise an arm under the previous test accrued 6 points but none under the current test. As a result, more claimants are being refused Employment and Support Allowance, either under the Work-related Activity Group or the Support Group. This has led to the welfare rights team being involved in lengthy appeals, which means claimants waiting up to nine months to be heard. In the meantime the team have had to ensure some kind of income maintenance was still in place for claimants while the appeal was pending.

The House of Commons Work and Pensions Committee (2011) investigated the whole process of migration, from Incapacity Benefit to Employment and Support Allowance. Their findings were highly critical of the process, in particular Atos Healthcare and Jobcentre Plus in their administration of the system. The extent to which the system was failing can be seen by the amount of appeals that were lodged from October 2008 to August 2009: 209,200 people were found to be fit for work and 68,500 appeals were lodged; to date, of the appeals heard, 40 per cent have resulted in a successful appeal. Further evidence taken by the Committee suggested that taken on a yearly basis and using 2010 as an example, some £50 million would be spent on WCA appeals. It is also clear from the evidence that even if a person wins their appeal, they are subjected to another round of assessments for their fitness for work. This is a continuous process, causing added stress to claimants, as Mind (2012) and other representatives of service users have pointed out. Often when the reassessment is made, the original decision of the appeal and the information given is not passed on to the assessors. The Committee also took evidence from service users, highlighting the difficulties with this process:

> A number of claimants told us of similar experiences. One woman wrote that "Each time I fail a WCA and have to go through the appeals process it knocks me back further from my goal of being fit enough to find work in the future." Another said it is "appalling that people who've gone through the appeals process and have had their original WCA overturned, then have to go through it all again, in a matter of weeks or months". (House of Commons Work and Pensions Committee, 2011)

The Committee was also highly critical of the service provided by Atos Healthcare, which they observed had fallen below the standard claimants should expect. This failure has contributed significantly to mistrust of the whole process. On the positive side they recognise that the decision-making process is also showing signs of improvement, with more decisions on work capability being 'got right the first time'. However, the Committee looked forward to Harrington's (2011) second independent review, which indeed highlighted some further improvements, but still recognised that there were significant problems. As Harrington concluded, there was still a culture within Atos Healthcare and Jobcentre Plus of passing and failing claimants, rather than providing the right kind of assessment to help claimants into work or providing the necessary support if they were unable to do so:

> There is an obvious need to support fully people who are unable to work through ill health or a disability. However, there is also a need to move away from concepts of "passing" or "failing" a WCA which are unhelpful and often cloud the evidence linking health and work. A fair and effective WCA will help in this respect, as well as providing a more cost effective system than is currently in operation. (Harrington, 2011, p 81)

In response to the many criticisms of the Work Capability Assessment the DWP has instituted a number of changes including:

- bringing in additional providers to carry out assessments other than Atos;
- directing Atos Healthcare to put in place a quality improvement plan to improve the quality of written reports following assessments;
- introduce measures to retrain and re-evaluate all Atos healthcare professionals. (DWP, 2013b)

The realisation by the DWP that it needs to refine its processes is clear; however it has not fully met some of the key criticisms levelled at the process by many of the groups mentioned earlier that represent those claimants affected. In particular, the assumption of capability that does not adequately account for a person's incapacity for many work roles and activities will continue to be a much-contested area. In addition it would seem appropriate to improve the appeals process and require claimants to be represented, given that the success rate of appeals improves significantly when trained advisers represent claimants.

Implications for social work

Although I have not been able to cover every aspect of the transition from Incapacity Benefit to Employment and Support Allowance, I have tried to outline some of the general problems that may be relevant for service users and social workers alike. The process of transition is not one that is designed to enable service users to find the most appropriate benefit for them. The approach needs to be understood within the general context of financial stringency and a belief that there are many people claiming Incapacity Benefit who are work-shy and who therefore 'scrounge' off the system. This culture is something that the House of

Commons Work and Pensions Committee (2011) felt was highly detrimental to providing a fair and accessible service. Individuals and families experiencing this process will therefore require a lot of support in helping them prepare for the assessment process and in presenting their evidence. In addition, if individuals are deemed fit for work or wrongly placed in the work-related category, then they will, again, need much support to help them through the appeals process. This is clearly a more specialised field, and social workers will be well advised to contact the local welfare rights office or the local Citizens' Advice Bureau to enable further support for the initial application and the appeal if required.

Although figures suggest that 40 per cent of appeals have been successful to date, the proportion that may be successful could be much higher if qualified welfare rights workers were involved; for example, Neath and Port Talbot Welfare Rights Unit (Hankins, 2012) report a success rate of 90 per cent. It would also seem appropriate for social workers to work with UNISON, their union, and local organisations such as Mind or the Citizens' Advice Bureau in helping provide information that can feed into the ongoing campaigns against these measures.

Impact of Universal Credit

Brewer et al (2012) have produced a preliminary analysis of the likely winners and losers as a result of the introduction of the Universal Credit scheme. From the analysis, not everyone on low incomes will benefit from these changes. The analysis assumes full take-up of benefits under the old regime and under Universal Credit. Overall, out of some 6.4 million families, 1.4 million will lose out. Universal Credit will benefit poorer families rather than those relatively well off; those in the lower six tenths of the income distribution will gain, and those in the top four tenths will lose out. On average, couples with children will gain more than couples without children and single adults without children. But, as the analysis makes clear, within all family types there will be winners and losers. Take-up will be increased under Universal Credit which is welcome, but at a cost for some claimants who may no longer qualify as they had done under the previous system.

Given our discussion regarding work incentives, will Universal Credit deliver on this? Incentives under this scheme will be strengthened for low-earning singletons and primary earners in couples. On the negative side, incentives will be weakened for potential second earners in couples as their Universal Credit will be reduced more quickly if they enter work than exists under the previous system. Universal Credit will also have a greater impact than the previous system as it will apply to work of less than 16 hours and to those without children.

Social work and a living wage

The overwhelming thrust of the Coalition government's social security policy as evidenced in the WRA 2012 is to activate claimants into work. A major plank of this approach is 'the benefit cap' that came into force as a pilot in London in

April 2013, highlighted at the beginning of this chapter. This policy has strong echoes of less eligibility. The aim is to make work pay by cutting total benefits to the average wage, that is, £26,000 per annum. Yet 84 per cent of households have an income of less than £26,000 (Cribb et al, 2012); therefore many of the households that will suffer from the benefit cap will have no opportunity to earn more in work than what they would receive in benefit. Thus if the government wanted to make work 'pay' by cutting benefits further there is nothing in the proposals that would prevent governments from capping benefits to, say, 60 per cent of median household income, which, as mentioned earlier, is the official poverty line.

The Resolution Foundation (2012) report into living standards is sceptical about future income growth from employment, and therefore many claimants whom social workers may come into contact with will face an extended period on relatively low wages, which will require assistance from Universal Credit. The Resolution Foundation (2012) calculated that for the group of families earning between £10,000 to £47,000, living standards over the period 2002-08 advanced by £143 a year; the interesting fact about this was that this advance, such as it is, was achieved not by an increase in male earnings, which actually fell by £610, but was achieved by an increase in women's earnings and tax credits (tax credits accounted for the majority of the increase). In future, this group of families will experience income decline so that by the second half of the decade families will have less than in 2000.

The decline in the share of income that labour receives is an international phenomenon so that in the 1990s, labour share was 66 per cent; by the late 2000s it was 61.7 per cent.

> Globalisation, financialisation and the decline of worker bargaining power are commonly suggested to be potential causes, though isolating causes for macroeconomic phenomena like this is difficult. (Resolution Foundation, 2012, p 24)

Although income from wages has reduced for those families identified earlier, this needs to be compared to the incomes of the UK's highest earners:

> After a brief dip from 2001 to 2003, average incomes in the top 0.1% of the UK income distribution accelerated upwards rapidly. Average incomes among the top 0.1% grew 65% in real terms from 2003 to 2007, an annual rate of 13.4% a year, easily the most rapid period of growth in the past 100 years. This ran alongside annual income growth of 1.6% for the entire bottom 90% of the population. (Resolution Foundation, 2012, p 25)

Given the evidence presented in this chapter, the future remains bleak for many service users living in poverty. The assumption that work will lift people out of poverty is highly questionable. A combination of economic austerity feeding into lower levels of social security benefit across all claimant groups is likely to further reinforce and increase the numbers of people living in poverty.

Summary

In this chapter we have explored the Coalition government's reforms of the social security system. We have shown how the Coalition government has introduced its reforms against a backdrop of one of the severest downturns in the global economy since the 1930s. The thrust of these reforms have been two-fold:

- to ensure that the government's economic policy of retrenchment is not compromised;
- to attempt to 'make work pay' for those on benefit.

Overall, these changes will have mixed results. In terms of incentives to work, different groups will benefit, or not, in different ways, so the impact of these policies will be uneven. The Coalition government is eager to involve as many claimants as possible in the Work Programme. In the case of those with a disability, they are likely to experience a great deal of uncalled-for stress and frustration unless the arrangements to enable people back into the labour market are focused more on help and assistance than merely clearing as many people as possible from receipt of Employment and Support Allowance. In respect to claimants of working age, the focus of the reforms is to reduce benefits to force people into what will be, for many, low-wage employment, where they will be no better off than if they were claiming benefits.

Recommend reading

DWP (Department for Work and Pensions) (2011) *A new approach to child poverty: Tackling the causes of disadvantage and transforming families' lives*, Cm 8061, London: The Stationery Office.

Grover, C. (2010) 'Social security policy and vindictiveness', *Sociological Research Online*, vol 15, no 2, p 8 (www.socresonline.org.uk/15/2/8.html).

4

Service users and the experience of poverty

This chapter investigates the meaning of poverty from the perspective of service users. To work effectively in combating poverty, social workers need to understand how service users experience poverty and the intervention provided by social workers to alleviate it. By understanding the experiences of service users, social workers will have the opportunity to reflect on and develop their own practice in relation to poverty.

The definitions, measurements and theories of poverty, as Ridge (2009) argues, represent only a partial picture of what poverty means for people. As social workers we need to know the direct impact of poverty on people's everyday lives. Therefore, investigating service users' experiences, either through research or direct testimony, has a central role to play in enabling social workers to alleviate poverty.

Conventional accounts of poverty have usually been the preserve of experts and academics in the field of poverty studies. Very rarely do the voices of the poor surface (although, for an exception, see Beresford et al, 1999). Poverty is not only a lack of income, a lack of access to services, for example, but a human problem that moves people to despair and anger; it can also move them to want to change their lives and the lives of others for the better.

In considering the personal understanding and emotional impact of poverty, Krumer-Nevo (2005) defines this as 'life knowledge'; he argues that this category of knowledge challenges some of the standard preconceptions as to how people deal with hardship and how assistance might be given. He argues that people living in poverty are often considered to have only partial knowledge of their situation. Many people in poverty lack significant formal education beyond secondary school, and their way of life is often judged as confirming their lack of learning. By listening to the voices of the poor we can develop knowledge that is not alienated from the service user or detached from their experiences.

The experience of poverty

In communicating with people living in poverty, the language that social workers employ is of central importance. Using language that people may find demeaning or that minimises their situation serves to alienate them from any meaningful dialogue with those professionals using such language. As Heffernan (2006) argues, the meanings we attach to words reveal the underlying values and attitudes about the things to which we are referring (see also Pugh, 1996). One of the ways individuals or groups who are in powerful positions, such as social workers, preserve their power is through the vehicle of language; as a consequence, the choice of words used can oppress those without power. McKendrick (2102) argues that the language that politicians, researchers and professionals use can serve to alienate the poor from the rest of society, a process of 'othering' the poor. For example, the term 'hard-working families' is often used in comparison to people living on social security benefit, implying that people in poverty are 'work-shy'. This can also be the case in using the word 'poverty' itself. As studies show, it is a very sensitive term and needs to be used with caution in relation to people who experience it (Beresford et al, 1999; Office of the Children's Commissioner, 2011; McKendrick, 2012). Service users in Beresford et al's study did not perceive themselves as 'poor' (see also Athwal et al, 2011); on the whole, they preferred not to use the word. Part of the reason is the stigma attached to such a term, which is conveyed powerfully by this service user:

> 'If you are poor … you are socially worse – you are literally socially worse, but even as a person, quality of character, it's automatically "you're poor" therefore you steal or may steal.' (quoted in Beresford et al, 1999, p 64)

Service users also understand the relative nature of poverty, particularly in relation to people from poorer countries. Therefore it is common for service users to describe people in the 'third world' as poor. A recent study by Athwal et al (2011, p 11) highlights how service users in Bradford understood poverty in relative terms:

> '… most people within our Bengali community, if you ask them about poverty, what they would say, as long as you've got a roof on your head and you can feed yourself three times then you're not in poverty … when you say to anybody in here [the community centre] what is poverty automatically you have an image of … a family in Bangladesh, people begging on the streets … or even here … homeless people.'

White interviewees also referred to the concept of relative poverty as compared to people in other countries:

> '… I wouldn't say I am living in poverty – people who live abroad in third world countries have poverty. We've got a roof over our heads and I've got food in my belly, they haven't – that's what I class as poverty, but I am still in poverty because the money that we have isn't enough to live on….' (quoted in Athwal et al, 2011, p 12)

When adults talk about poverty they often use metaphor to describe their feelings in this regard. Underlid (2007, p 69), in his study of poor people's perceptions of poverty in Norway, reported on Steinar's perception (a service user):

'Like you're out there swimming and on the verge of drowning.'

Or another service user, Triene's:

'It's like you're climbing a very steep mountain.... Then it starts slipping away from under your feet.' (quoted in Underlid, 2007, p 69)

The use of metaphor is not constrained to the poor living in the affluent parts of the globe:

'Poverty is like living in jail, living under bondage, waiting to be free.' (Jamaican man living in poverty)

'For a poor person everything is terrible – illness, humiliation, shame. We are cripples [sic]; we are afraid of everything; we depend on everyone. No one needs us. We are like garbage that everyone wants to get rid of. (A blind woman from Tiraspol, Moldova) (quoted in Narayan and Petesch, 2002, p 64)

However, children's responses can be more direct, as this study of children in Wales demonstrates:

'When other people have money they don't make fun of them but when the other people go up the shops with their mothers if he just looks at them then you feel down and bit and sad. Because they're happy and we're sad. I feel very sad when my mum has no money because I can't buy anything.' (quoted in Crowley and Vulliamy, 2011, p 24)

Exercise

Given the importance of the language that social workers use in relation to poverty, make a list of terms that you feel would be less stigmatising to service users.

Commentary

Given the sensitive nature of the terminology used, it is important that you can speak about a service user's circumstances openly and honestly without making them feel stigmatised. This means avoiding euphemisms such as 'financially challenged' even though service users may have read this term in the press or heard it on the broadcast media. Terms should be shared with service users that avoid unnecessary embarrassment or harm. McKendrick (2012) describes the challenge as that, on the one hand, we describe poverty in a way that is respectful of service users while it is also sensitive to how these descriptions may be received by them. However, we should not just be content with this, given that the use of language can be both negative and positive in its connotations. In describing poverty we challenge the negative assumptions so that we can talk with service users in a way that is positive and therefore respects their experience. In essence the approach in communicating with people who are poor should be the same as any communication with service users, which should have at its core a fundamental respect for the person. So, for example, in clarifying the situation of a service user it would be helpful to use the term 'a person experiencing poverty'; in describing the area the person may live in, if it is an area with a large number of people living in poverty, then 'areas with poverty' or 'areas with deprivation' seem the most respectful; and in describing living in this situation of poverty, then McKendrick suggests 'living on a low income'.

This may sound as if we are playing with words, but as the research shows, the potential for individual support of service users in social work terms is compromised when people quite rightly wish to reject a spurious identity that is seen as demeaning or not applicable to them, regardless of their actual living situation (Ravensbergen and VanderPlaat, 2010). The feeling of being labelled as poor and the stigma that people often feel from being defined in this way can be illuminated by the example of free school meals (FSM). Stigma is therefore not just a function of our personal interactions and use of language, but is also reinforced by the policy process itself. Encouragingly, as the study below highlights, the impact of stigma can be significantly alleviated by policies that are more inclusive of the population.

Of the approximately 1.1 million children who are entitled to receive a FSM, Holford (2012) found about 300,000 children entitled to FSMs are either not registered, or are registered but fail to take it up, costing their parents up to £400 per year. However, in five areas in Scotland, FSMs were temporarily made available to *all* children in the first three years of primary school (ages 5-8). Take-up of school meals increased among non–FSM-registered pupils by 14 percentage points, from 38 per cent. Among FSM-registered individuals, for whom school meals were *always* free, take-up rose by 5 percentage points, from 86 per cent. This occurred despite the scheme providing no financial incentive for the latter group to change their behaviour.

Holford concluded that this increase in take-up of FSM by those always entitled to FSM showed a positive peer effect. Children registered for FSM were more likely to participate because a greater proportion of other students in the school were doing so. These findings can be generalised to schools never exposed to universal entitlement. The magnitude of the effect is such that in a typical school, a 10-percentage point rise in peer group take-up would reduce non-participation by almost a quarter.

For Holford the effects of stigma can be reduced through the participation of all pupils in FSM. Interestingly the reduction in stigma is due to the reduced probability that an FSM participant will be eating separately from friends; this is a signal that a school meal is of sufficient quality to make it popular with all pupils. For social workers who may be working in partnership with schools, then there may be some useful lessons learned. Even though the universal provision of FSM may not be immediately possible, schools should ensure that classmates taking school meals and packed lunches can eat at the same time and eat together. Local authorities can also ensure that FSM-registered pupils remain anonymous when obtaining their school lunch. Finally, at a national level, policy should be directed for the provision of FSM at year groups within the most deprived schools, rather than singling out individuals.

Policies aimed at promoting inclusion of the poor and that are organised around universalist principles can be successful in reducing the worst aspects of stigma. Unfortunately, governments across the world are heavily influenced by neo-liberal ideology that gives primacy to individual economic interests in which the market and commerce predominate over social solidarity. As individuals within this system we are seen as consumers and our identity is often tied to consumption. The fuel for this system is money, which, as Underlid (2005) argues, confers self-esteem on those who have it and for those unsuccessful in acquiring money, its opposite.

> In a society of consumers, the life projects of whom are based on consumer choices, the poor are non-starters. (Underlid, 2005, p 277)

As Bauman (2005) has argued, once a society defines itself and others by how it consumes, then to be a successful consumer is to be 'normal'. Those who are unable to consume are therefore excluded and marked as social failures who have no social function or worth as they have no means to enhance their membership of such a consumerist society. This has its consequences; for example, children from poor families who are unable to wear the 'right' kind of clothes to school may be subject to bullying face to face or through cyberbullying. A recent study (Munro, 2011) identified key groups at risk of cyberbullying, all of whom constitute groups seen as 'others', of whom children in receipt of FSMs make up a significant number. Vulnerable groups include children with special educational needs (SEN), children in receipt of FSMs, children from black and minority ethnic (BME) groups, children of Gypsy-Roma, Traveller or Irish Heritage, European and East European groups, children from Chinese groups and children of mixed ethnicity.

As a consequence, service users may be highly distrustful of social workers who have considerable power over them and who act as gatekeepers of resources that they may need. This can be characterised by a certain reticence to engage with those who have potentially so much control over their daily lives. This distrust may be further compounded by the way service users report that those professionals they do come into contact with seem indifferent to their plight. In general it is not surprising that service users will not welcome state professionals as partners in trying to alleviate their poverty (Ravensbergen and VanderPlaat, 2010). Social workers who therefore wish to engage effectively will have to work extremely hard to develop the trust of service users. Working in partnership with service users will therefore be challenging for social workers as long as they are seen as exclusively representing the state.

The consequences of living in poverty

In this section some of the findings from research with service users who describe the impact of poverty on their lives are presented. In order to do this we look at different dimensions of poverty, including:

• poverty in relation to social networks and relationships
• poverty in relation to lack of income
• poverty in relation to exclusion from valued activities.

In many ways, as identified below, these dimensions merge into one another as a lack of income inevitably strains relationships within families and also impairs individuals' and families' abilities to participate in valued activities.

Dimensions of poverty

At the social level the interaction between poor people and those who see themselves as better off induces social isolation. Lane (2009) shows how the reaction of the non-poor can be highly selective and discriminatory, evoking from them either anger or pity. On the one hand, anger divorces those better off from the poor and places blame on the poor for their fate, while pity evokes a distancing effect in which the better off may respond in an individual way but fail to link the fate of the poor to wider distributional issues in society. Dorey (2010) reinforces this view as, in income distribution terms, the top 10 per cent own 100 times more than the bottom 10 per cent. Yet there is remarkably little public concern or anger about inequality and poverty. Concern for the poor has declined in recent years, and there is an increased prevalence that poverty is caused by laziness and lack of self-motivation. Indeed, more apprehension seems to focus on the middle classes being stretched financially rather than overall levels of poverty (Park et al, 2012). This lack of understanding increases the distance between the poor and the rest of the population.

In assessing the impact on social networks for poor people it is important to recognise the positive contribution played by families and close friends in providing support. Walker et al (2008), in their study of children of single parents, identify the role grandparents play in providing childcare to enable single parents to go to work or go for job interviews. In addition, grandparents can provide essential items of clothing, and other items such as toys that the single parent would not be able to provide otherwise. This process is referred to as 'social network capital' which points to the benefits that households gain from linking with others to enable mutual help and assistance. Social network capital can be important in helping people to escape persistent poverty, but social networking can be costly and is therefore no panacea. Not all households find it worthwhile to link with others and some will be rebuffed through further exclusion by those within their own neighbourhood; for example, families with a child with a disability may experience such isolation. A report by Contact a Family (2011) surveyed over 1,000 such families. Sixty-five per cent felt frequent isolation, with 52 per cent reporting being discriminated against. In addition, the usefulness of social networks depends on the structure of the economy in which the poor reside. In some settings well-targeted public transfers and the support of agencies such as voluntary, community groups and social services may help the creation of new social network capital and therefore enable the amelioration of and therefore alleviate poverty (Chantarat and Barrett, 2011).

Families experience stress in managing expectations, particularly between parents and children. Athwal et al (2011) identified the stress placed on parents, particularly mothers, when children asked for something that they could not provide. The response to children's wishes varied in relation to which ethnic group was being interviewed, but all groups voiced feelings of sadness and guilt at not being able to provide for their children in this way; this led some mothers to take out loans in order to meet their children's expectations:

> 'I will not let my children miss out. I would rather go get a loan and take the consequences afterwards.' (White woman, focus group participant) (quoted in Athwal et al, 2011, p 14)

This is a common reaction by parents, in particular when celebrations such as Christmas or Eid come around or loved ones' birthdays. Recent evidence suggests that more families are now getting into debt to pay for essentials. Contact a Family (2012) surveyed 2,000 families with children with disabilities, and found that:

- a third (29 per cent) had taken out a loan – 39 per cent for food and heating;
- a quarter of loans were from quick cash schemes or from loan sharks;
- one in five (21 per cent) had been threatened with court action for failing to keep up with payments – the majority for missing utility bill payments (46 per cent).

Many poor parents only have access to very expensive forms of credit, for example, from loan companies, and many described problems with paying off debts and the often illegal attentions of aggressive creditors. Indeed, many credit agents target the more deprived areas, offering to lend money or sell high street vouchers. The more legitimate lenders such as high street banks were also seen as a problem in offering bank loans and credit cards, particularly to young people who were not able to manage the debt (Green, 2007).

Poverty has a negative impact on the poor in the area of transport – much access to leisure facilities and shopping is no longer easily accessible, with many shopping facilities and leisure facilities placed in out-of-town locations. This is problematic for those living in rural areas where access to public transport is more limited. The consequence of what can be called 'transport poverty' is that the opportunities to share social and leisure occasions with family and friends are severely limited. The effect of low income therefore acts to isolate the poor from their friends and family, and this is particularly the case in relation to family celebrations. In Athwal et al's (2011) study, participants said that they hid from friends when they could not go out through lack of money, and these feelings seemed to be expressed more often by men:

> 'I've got no life really, both of us, it is just, you know, doing what we have to do out of here then come back in and that's it, close doors, so weekend's pretty the same really, just stay in....' (White man)

> 'Socialising, I think that's one of the things.... Not having an income, to be around your friends ... you kind of don't want to be around people all the time, because of that feeling of, I don't know, not self-worth.... I don't want to feel like I'm reliant on people, I'm a man, I'm independent ... I'd say I'm a lot less sociable....' (African Caribbean man)

> '...The crowd that I have grown up with, some of them have got full-time jobs, some of them haven't got a job so we can't stick together because of money....' (Bangladeshi man) (Focus group participants) (quoted in Athwal et al, 2011, p 15)

In neighbourhoods with higher levels of people living on a low income, facilities in those neighbourhoods are sparse. As one boy observed:

> 'There ain't nothing to do round here. A sports centre would be good, swimming pool, football, badminton. But let's be realistic it ain't going to happen.' (Boy, 15, secondary school) (Urban focus group participant) (quoted in Walker et al, 2008, p 432)

As a consequence, children's activities are focused on the locality in which they live, which means that much of their time is spent either at home or on the streets, where they may be more vulnerable to crime. People on low incomes are around twice as likely to feel very unsafe walking alone in their area at night as those on above-average incomes (Palmer et al, 2006).

Living on a low income therefore involves a constant juggling of resources; Green's (2007) study showed participants voicing these problems in relation to paying for fuel. Participants described making choices between buying food and heating their homes or being fearful of using washing machines because of the impact on their fuel bills. The pressure on participants to afford even the basic necessities and the ability of maintaining a healthy diet was almost impossible:

'My GP asked me "are you eating healthily?", but how can I afford to do that?!' (Asylum seeker group, Glasgow) (quoted in Green, 2007, p 18)

'The recent recession and all the cutbacks have hit me hard. My bank account is never in the pluses, always in the minuses, so that is a constant struggle in itself. I've cut back to the bare bones and still the government wants to cut more. My son misses out on some school trips, which I just can't afford. Sometimes I go without a meal so that my son can eat.' (Low-income parent) (quoted in Save the Children, 2012b, p 4)

The survey above (Save the Children, 2012b) found that parents living in poverty were more likely to have avoided paying bills (40 per cent) compared to parents on higher incomes (11 per cent). The difficulties parents face is beginning to move up the income ladder as parents (58 per cent) on modest incomes report having to struggle to maintain a basic standard of living. Parents were asked to think about their spending on food over the past year. Large numbers of families across different income groups reported cutting back on buying fruit and vegetables:

'A year or so ago, we literally relied on any money we raised at car boot sales to pay for food for the week. Some weeks weren't too bad; others were dire. The British weather decided how we lived that week (when it rained, the turnout at car boot sales fell).' (Low-income parent) (Save the Children, 2012b, p 4)

Fuel poverty

A household is considered to be living in fuel poverty if it spends more than 10 per cent of its annual income on heating, lighting, cooking etc. In 2010 the most recent available figures showed 4 million households living in fuel poverty. Throughout the previous decade numbers had stayed around 1.5 million, but in 2009 they rose to 4.5 million, declining slightly in 2010. In relation to the total number of households in the UK, these figures represent 18 per cent of total households living in fuel poverty (DECC, 2012). The key determinants of fuel poverty are lack of income, increasing fuel prices and fuel consumption. In reducing fuel poverty the crucial factor is increasing a household's income. For social workers this means using the assessment process to identify if a household may be experiencing fuel poverty and to look at ways of increasing the income of households and/or to enable the more efficient use of fuel through exploring ways to insulate the home. Differences occur between devolved administrations as to how fuel poverty may be defined; for example, in Scotland there is a more stringent interpretation of a satisfactory heating regime for pensioners, the long-term sick and disabled households. This means that these groups are assumed to require a higher temperature to reach an adequate standard of warmth in their homes. However, as DECC (2012) shows, the reason for the rise in fuel poverty has been the significant increase in energy prices:

> Between 2004 and 2009, energy prices increased: domestic electricity prices rose by over 75%, and gas prices increased by over 122% over the period. This led to the rise in fuel poverty seen over this period. The overall effect of price rises since 2004 has far outweighed the impact of increasing incomes and energy efficiency. (DECC, 2012, p 12)

Who are the 'fuel poor'?

As mentioned earlier, rises in the income of households reduce the numbers living in fuel poverty, and not surprisingly the lowest 20 per cent of households by income account for 74 per cent of those households living in fuel poverty. By employment status 50 per cent of households with an unemployed member are fuel poor, while 30 per cent of households with a member who is economically inactive are fuel poor (for example, a retired person, or someone deemed unfit for work). In terms of the total numbers of those in fuel poverty, 50 per cent of these households include either a couple or a single person over the age of 60. Nineteen per cent involve a couple with dependent children and 9 per cent a single parent with dependent children. In terms of energy use, 29 per cent of fuel-poor households are in properties that do not use gas. No figures are given in terms of 'race' or gender (see DECC, 2012), but given that women and people from minority ethnic groups generally experience lower incomes than the rest of population, it is likely that fuel poverty will be experienced at a disproportionate rate for these groups. The impact of fuel poverty at its starkest is explored by Hills (2012, p 10), who points out:

> From a health and well-being perspective: living at low temperatures as a result of fuel poverty is likely to be a significant contributor not just to the excess winter deaths that occur each year (a total of 27,000 each year over the last decade in England and Wales), but to a much larger number of incidents of ill-health and demands on the National Health Service and a wider range of problems of social isolation and poor outcomes for young people.

This view has been further supported by O'Brien (2012), who detailed the health impacts of fuel poverty as a result of poorly heated households. These include:

- higher mortality risk in older people
- reduced overall physical, mental and emotional wellbeing
- increased circulatory and respiratory disease in adults

- increased risk of falls, mental health illness, social isolation
- increases in hospital admissions, asthma/exacerbation of symptoms in children, and minor illnesses such as coughs and colds.

Prepayment meters

Many service users therefore struggle to pay for their energy. This can result in disconnection in some instances, or energy companies may suggest that a prepayment meter is issued. Modern prepayment meters have a failsafe amount of additional energy capacity to allow for when a person runs out of money, but this is minimal. For people trying to manage on a small budget, meters do have some advantages:

- energy bills are broken down into a series of (arbitrarily) small payments;
- they often (but not always) come with a lower-than-standard tariff;
- there is instant information feedback, allowing prepayment customers to better monitor their energy use.

However, they also come with one major disadvantage – when credit runs out, so the supply of energy stops. For social workers advising service users whether to use prepayment meters, this poses some serious dilemmas. For families with children, people with disabilities or older people, do they potentially face a sudden cut-off of energy through lack of immediate cash with its attendant risks, for example, older people suffering from hypothermia? These problems have not stemmed the use of prepayment meters:

> To date approximately 3.6 million households (14%) use pre-payment meters to pay for their electricity; 2.6 million households (10%) use them to pay for their gas consumption; and 2.3 million households (9%) use them to pay for both: electricity and gas. (Brutscher, 2011, p 7)

Brutscher (2011) found, for example, with electricity prepayment meters, that the household was more likely to:

- have a female household head
- be significantly less likely to be economically active
- be significantly more likely to rent their home than households without a prepayment meter.

Where households have electricity and gas meters, the household experiences an intensification of these characteristics, so that they are:

- (even) more likely to have a female household head
- (even) less likely to be economically active

• (even) more likely to rent their home than households with an electricity meter only.

The Coalition government is reducing help for those who may experience trouble meeting their energy bills. The total budget for Warm Front (a scheme to provide free insulation to homes) in 2011/12 and 2012/13 was £210 million; the scheme ended in January 2013. In addition, new eligibility criteria from 2011 will result in fewer households being eligible for a grant. Proposals that will take the place of Warm Front do not match the previous scheme in terms of affordability for the poorest. A 'Green Deal' was proposed from late 2012, to allow consumers to pay for energy efficiency improvements through their energy bills. Energy suppliers were required to spend £250 million in 2011/12, rising to £310 million by 2014/15, providing assistance with energy costs to vulnerable customers. In addition, uplift to winter fuel payments introduced in 2008 was being withdrawn from 2011/12, resulting in a reduction of £50 to £100 for eligible households. If the current cutbacks in help to the poorest remain, then the narratives identified below are likely to become more desperate as people begin to struggle with increased costs, with a reduction in available help.

Narratives of fuel poverty

These figures are given further meaning when we listen to those living in fuel poverty. In this regard we can begin to understand the often difficult choices individuals and families have to make, for example, between maintaining heating in winter or eating a hot meal:

> 'Winter was really bad – we had ice on the inside of our windows, the whole way up to the top of the window. My main thing with not having an awful lot of money is that I'm afraid to put the heating on. I've cut back on absolutely everything, I've really cutback.' (Debbie, mother of one) (quoted in Save the Children, 2012c, p 3)

> 'I only have a bath before school on a Sunday night and one on a Wednesday night, because hot water is expensive. The boys carry around their bed covers in the house and sit downstairs with them in the day because it's so cold. We all do it when it's really cold because the gas isn't on all day. We have to go to the shop to buy tokens for the meter to heat the living room.' (Stacey, 16) (quoted in Save the Children, 2012c, p 1)

> 'I'm really panicking about the rise in gas and electricity prices – and food is now a problem for me too. I am struggling to put food on the table after paying the bills.' (Energy Action Scotland group, West Lothian) (quoted in Green, 2007, p 19)

'I now buy food and bring it home – cooked chicken and things like that, because I'm scared to use the oven because I know it costs too much money. I only use the washing machine twice a week because I'm scared of what it costs.' (Refugee group, Glasgow) (quoted in Green, 2007, p 19)

'If we pay more for our bills then that means that my parents can't buy me any resources for my learning....' (Mahima, age 10)

'I worry. I can't put the heating on like everybody else can. Some people put it on at six in the morning at and leave it on all day so the house stays at a constant temperature, but because we can't, the house gets cold. If my son or I get sick, the asthma just flares up, and if it's not controlled quite quickly either he or I will end up in hospital.' (quoted in Save the Children, 2012c, p 4)

Summary

This chapter has identified, through the voices of service users, the daily struggle that they experience in order to provide the basics for their survival. Contrary to much media opinion, the testimonies presented here show a determination to live in as responsible a way as possible in order that some modicum of dignity is salvaged from what is a desperate situation. In listening to the voices of poor people it is argued that this provides a first step for social workers in both understanding the impact of poverty and also in providing the first steps towards working in partnership with the poor.

For social workers to respond sensitively to what service users tell them about their experience of poverty it requires them to not only actively listen but to give direction and to shape their practice. What informs the overall direction of their response will therefore be their commitment to social justice. The following chapter identifies the centrality of social work ethics and in particular social justice in order to shape social workers practice to the needs of service users.

Recommended reading

Beresford, P., Green, D., Lister, R. and Woodward, K. (1999) *Poverty first hand: Poor people speak for themselves*, London: Child Poverty Action Group.

Green, M. (2007) *Voices of people experiencing poverty in Scotland: Everyone matters?*, York: Joseph Rowntree Trust.

5

Social work and poverty: ethics and practice

The starting point for effective practice in ameliorating poverty is to build on the knowledge of service users' experiences of poverty and their perceptions of the social services that they have come into contact with. Thus, for social workers wishing to work in an anti-oppressive way, then they need to:

• work in partnership
• work to empower service users
• use statutory intervention as a last resort (Parrott, 2010).

Given the ethical underpinnings discussed previously, it is important to recognise that in any work with service users a clear and systematic process is being undertaken. By adopting a systematic process we can maintain a focus on those aspects of a service user's situation that they feel is important, and avoid drift in terms of the direction in which the social work intervention will lead. A systematic process therefore involves assessment, a plan, intervention and evaluation:

Assessment: investigate and analyse the expressed needs of the service user, making sure that any information obtained is valid and relevant to the service user's situation and follows the value of confidentiality. The process to involve the service user seeks to draw out the strengths that service users bring while helping to identify particular issues that need to be worked on.

Plan: agree a course of action with the service user; this means enabling the service user to develop a strategy that is acceptable to them and that they can be involved in realising.

Intervene: enable the service user to use their capabilities in a way that will lead to achievable outcomes. Agree on what they can do and what you will do, review progress in terms of the goals set on a regular basis. Agree on how much time will be devoted to the task.

Evaluate: discuss what has been achieved, make sure that you both understand what has been achieved so that the service user can assess for him or herself what may be needed to be addressed in the future.

For the purposes of this chapter, only the stages of assessment and planning are covered given that within the confines of the case study discussed later, we cannot discuss with any degree of accuracy the likely scenarios that may emerge from the intervention and evaluation stages.

Working in partnership

When social workers engage with people living in poverty they will invariably be working with people who have been referred to them for some other reason than being poor. It may be that they have problems coping at home due to disability or mental health problems, they may be experiencing difficulties in parenting their children or their children may be experiencing difficulties at home, or any number of other reasons. For service users, their first contact with social workers is likely to be highly stressful and they may well be mistrustful of social workers' intentions. This mistrust may undermine any positive intervention attempted by social workers. It is not just confined to service users currently receiving services, but is reflected in the population at large. A recent Ipsos MORI survey found that 60 per cent of respondents said they would trust social workers to tell the truth; this was a similar trust rate for the police, who scored 63 per cent. But compared with other public professions, the rating of social work did not compare well – doctors achieved a trust rate of 88 per cent, professors, 74 per cent, teachers, 81 per cent and judges, 72 per cent (Ipsos MORI, 2011).

Strier and Binyamin's (2010) review charted the troubled relationship between service users and social workers, observing that service users experience social services as bureaucratic, dehumanising and oppressive. As noted in previous chapters, current policy in the UK is doing nothing to help in this regard. Wiggan (2012) studied the discourse around some of the preparatory documents that set out the subsequent policy towards the social security reforms mentioned earlier. He argues that in such documents as the UK Coalition government's 2010 Green Paper, *21st century welfare* (DWP, 2010b), and the White Paper, *Universal Credit: Welfare that works* (DWP, 2010c), the central theme is to promote a discourse about social security that supports and restates the primacy of neo-liberal economic orthodoxy. This discourse assumes that poverty will be reduced by creating an institutional environment that restores to people living in poverty a sense of personal responsibility over their lives. Central to this is encouraging the poor into work by promoting their personal competence and responsibility and relegating their dependence on social security payments and welfare services. Blaming the poor for their poverty and forcibly moving them into work does not create a climate where trusting and respectful relationships can flourish.

As Strier and Binyamin (2010) argue, partnership working is a complex process in which social workers and service users explore ways in which they can work together. The differential power that exists between them must be recognised in order to develop mutuality and respectfulness so that a more equal working relationship can be achieved. This can only be developed through the social work organisation encouraging a climate in which equal and respectful relationships can grow.

Exercise

In order to achieve the goals of partnership working, consider the case study below and identify:

1. What are the main issues?
2. What principles would you employ to work with Jane?
3. What strengths does Jane bring to this problem that she faces?
4. What are the implications for you wanting to work in an anti-oppressive way to counter Jane's experience of poverty?

Case study

Jane is a 44-year-old woman, with two children – David aged 18 and Nicholas aged 11. Four years ago her husband died suddenly while at work, and she is now a single parent. Jane has been made redundant as the company she was working for as an administration officer has closed down and 'moved its operation', as the redundancy letter explained, to its other factory in Poland. The family live in privately rented accommodation in the middle of Kensington in London. Jane comes from a close-knit family who live near Jane and she has become particularly close to her mother and father-in-law since her husband's death.

Jane obtains alternative employment relatively quickly, but increasingly has to take time off work as David has profound learning disabilities and is about to move from school into college, which is resulting in significant behavioural problems at school to such an extent that the school is finding it increasingly difficult to manage his outbursts. This results in him coming home to 'cool off', which means Jane has to remain at home some times and take time off work. She feels this is important as her relationship with David is strong and she has always been able to parent David effectively when he experiences behavioural problems.

Jane is eventually dismissed from her job through having to take too much time off work to care for David and to attend the many meetings that his school have called as a means of trying to manage David's behaviour.

Jane is feeling increasingly stressed and visits her GP who prescribes her a course of tranquillizers. Jane feels that she is becoming increasingly isolated, seeing few people other than her children, and this begins to depress her further. She misses the social contact at work and her financial position begins to weigh heavily on her as she struggles to meet her energy bills. This is an increasing problem now that she and David are spending increasing amounts of time at home. Jane has begun to meet other parents with children who have similar behavioural problems to David via a local support group organised by the local community centre.

Nicholas is finding that the stress at home means he spends increasing amounts of time on the street playing with his friends and tends to stay out until it's very late. In addition, he is finding the transition to secondary school difficult. While at school he is being teased, particularly about his brother who sometimes meets him at the end of school with Jane.

When Jane worked she paid for a number of items via a catalogue and also had a number of hire purchase agreements to pay for a television and cooker. She is now finding it impossible to meet these debts and eventually receives a letter saying that her cooker, television and vacuum cleaner are going to be repossessed by bailiffs.

Commentary

Jane's situation is one that social workers will find familiar. In working through the principles of partnership, it is therefore important to hear Jane recount her own story in her own words. This provides Jane with the opportunity to describe her situation in the way that she understands it. This is a necessary step in working with Jane to assess her situation. This is not to say that the social worker does not bring up any relevant issues but that the social worker asks Jane if she has considered all the relevant issues that the social worker identifies, as the interaction with Jane develops. Building on the narratives of service users in the previous chapter, it is crucial to be able to build a trusting relationship so that Jane does not experience the feelings of stigma and frustration that service users living in poverty have identified. At each stage of the process the social worker must continually appreciate and listen to the service user's concerns. This does not mean, however, that social workers avoid what may be considered by service users uncomfortable advice if this is required to prevent harm or a service user potentially being disadvantaged. Any observations made by the social worker must be considered advice (unless harm or an illegal act is involved) so that service users' autonomy can be maintained.

Having recognised some of the issues that have an impact on the social worker–service user relationship and the importance of gaining trust, we now look at the assessment process.

Assessment is at the heart of social work practice and as such provides a crucial step in determining with the service user the nature of the problems that they feel are important to them. The most appropriate form of assessment in relation to issues of poverty would therefore encourage service users to assess their issues together with the social worker. Smale et al (1993) identify three approaches to assessment:

- *The questioning model:* a process of fact-finding and collection of relevant information that the social worker then processes to produce a diagnosis of the situation. The social worker stands as the expert who produces a professional judgement.
- *The procedural model:* in this assessment, engagement with the service user is determined by what procedures and policies the agency that employs the social worker deems necessary. The outcome is therefore to determine whether a person meets certain criteria for a service.

Given the testimonies of service users in the previous chapter, these two approaches may not be the best way to engage service users who experience poverty. It is likely that their experience of the social security system and its officials is likely to mirror this procedural model where any interaction is determined by the immediate policies of the social security system. Likewise, the questioning model may also reflect some aspects of the assessments that service users with disabilities may experience when being assessed as to their suitability to work where a designated assessor is required to make a judgement as to their suitability.

- *The exchange model:* Smale's final model is therefore a more appropriate form of assessment. People are viewed more as experts who can understand their own situation. What people express is a starting point for them to look at their own strengths to see how they can best alleviate the problems that they face. Service users themselves define their own problems and set out a plan to overcome them as long as they are legal and do not cause harm to others. It is important that service users who have had experiences where previously they may have been led through a process by an 'expert', or who are subject to quite intensive investigation of their circumstances, are given time to work through this process.

People living in poverty therefore require a more constructivist approach that builds on strengthening their abilities and talents, from a position of listening to their accounts to seeking positive solutions for themselves. This approach draws on the work of Fook (2012) and of Parton and O'Byrne (2000).

Living and surviving in poverty takes a great deal of skill and ingenuity, and these assets need to be valued and built on. The narratives in the previous chapter highlighted the sacrifices and hard choices people living in poverty have to make on a daily basis. In focusing on a person's strengths and coping capacity this can counter the stigma that people experience and give them the opportunity to have some control over their own situation. As Underlid (2005) has shown, within a Scandinavian context the interaction with officials from the social security system resulted in claimants feeling inadequate and shameful. In many respects their experiences of having their personal lives put under the microscopic gaze of officialdom left them feeling that their private life had been revealed for all to investigate, classify and pass judgement on. This is a version of what the French theorist Foucault called the 'medical gaze', the dehumanising process by which the medical profession's concern purely with a patient's body leads them to discount aspects of the patient's identity (Chambon et al, 1999).

Resilience theory can be useful here in understanding how those living in poverty can build on their strengths and value their achievements to date. Resilience refers to the ability to withstand or recover from often stressful situations. Stress, as understood here, refers to stress that is presented as feelings that are hard if not impossible to cope with. Most individuals, unless they live a totally uninspired life, experience stress and are able to overcome the challenge, for example of, bereavement and loss. It is in the context of people experiencing poverty that some of the 'normal' stresses in life can therefore become intolerable. This is not to say that people living in poverty are not resilient, but there is the potential for those people who experience poverty to face greater obstacles to dealing with these everyday stressors.

The building blocks in this process, therefore, reflect the principles of partnership and empowerment. The more that a person experiences a sense of security, the more that they see themselves as having self-worth, the more they can take control of their own lives. It is from this secure base that resilience can be built. Working with service users to see how they can develop and build such attributes provides a sense of hope and control that are important in building resilience (Parrott et al, 2008). An initial phase should be to value behaviour that exhibits resilience, such as maintaining social networks or continuing interests outside of a person's normal daily life. In working in an anti-oppressive way resilience needs to be understood across a number of levels. The personal level may build coping strategies and people's wellbeing through to social and cultural levels. For example, certain cultural practices and beliefs can strengthen resilience through to the wider social environment. Ungar et al (2004) identify the importance of an individual's relationship to their wider social and cultural environment in creating cultural and social pathways to resilience. They show the contribution of unique cultural contexts even in very challenging environments as their research looked at the resilience of Palestinian adolescents and their daily experiences of the conflict in Palestine.

Jane's assessment

In terms of Jane's story, it is likely that she will be feeling that she has few options to improve her life at the moment. The combination of material poverty and the stress that she is experiencing with regard to her children may leave her feeling that there is little that can be done. Therefore, in working with Jane, both the material and emotional concerns that she has expressed need to be assessed together. Jane begins to outline in more detail some of her problems, and these are now listed below:

- Jane lives in an area with high rental values and her Housing Benefit has been capped (see Chapter 3).
- In order to maintain living in her flat she is using money set aside for heating, lighting and for food.
- Her flat is not well insulated and in need of repair, which means further claims on her energy bills.
- Jane's feelings of depression means she no longer feels confident or energised to face her problems as well as she did before becoming ill.
- David's behavioural problems and his pending transition from his school environment to college is an added stressor when the school sends him home.

- Nicholas's transition to secondary school and his experience of bullying upsets Jane, especially when she experiences this first hand when she meets Nicholas from school.
- Nicholas staying away from the family home for long periods at night causes Jane to worry that he might be getting into trouble and mixing with what she calls the 'wrong crowd'.
- Jane's unemployment frustrates her as she has always worked, and apart from the money problems this brings, she also feels she should work as this provides an outlet from her problems at home.

Commentary

In identifying aspects of Jane's life which concern her it is important to validate what Jane is experiencing and feeling; it is also crucial to encourage Jane to look at her personal strengths and resources that have enabled her to cope in such difficult circumstances. This may be difficult for Jane to value at this stage and it may be necessary to support her in recognising her strengths. Therefore the social worker encourages Jane to look constructively at her own resilience and coping mechanisms. As a result of this dialogue she is able to recognise her:

- strong relationship with her mother and father-in-law
- skills as an office administrator
- ability to parent her children in very difficult circumstances
- contact with the support group
- determination to find work.

Plan

In responding to these challenges, Jane needs to decide what the most pressing problems are. She decides that her debts and living situation are clearly important issues alongside her depressed emotional state. She understands that these immediate challenges are interlinked, and with her agreement, the social worker decides to give these issues priority. Therefore the social worker suggests she contacts either her local welfare rights service that may be either run by the local authority or the local Citizens' Advice Bureau. This is crucial in enabling Jane to feel that she can begin to take control over her situation, a key building block in developing her resilience. Both these aspects of Jane's circumstances require an assessment as to the level of debt and the amount of current income she has.

Jane's relationship with David's school is also a key stressor for Jane, and the social worker agrees to contact the school and organise a meeting so that with their support, Jane can explore different options in managing David's behaviour. Clearly, given the reasons for Jane's recent termination of employment, any chance of maintaining future employment rests with the school taking a more active role by finding different ways to care for David rather than just sending him home.

Nicholas staying out may be a function of the increased amount of time Jane has to spend with David, and therefore Jane may like to explore ways in which she can spend more time with

Nicholas. It may be possible through the support group that parents could begin to provide activities for David at the community centre to enable Jane to give more time to Nicholas.

Commentary

In working with people living in poverty a variety of different issues merge into one another and therefore require social workers to recognise the way material and emotional issues interplay to create the kinds of stress that Jane is experiencing. With the brief overview of an initial response to Jane's situation, it is clear that the social worker involved needs to provide both encouragement and support to enable Jane to begin to think of a way out of her current situation. While there are some things in this situation that are amenable to some immediate response, there are other aspects of this intervention that are not easily susceptible that refer to wider institutional and structural issues, which are reflected in Jane's predicament. As Thompson (2001) argues in relation to working in an anti-oppressive way, the farther away a problem's resolution lies from the service user, the harder it is to seek an immediate resolution. Such problems that have their cause in, for example, the WRA 2012 and the introduction of the benefit cap, means that until this policy is changed, any resolution will mean finding extra income for Jane that offsets her loss of benefits. While this may be possible if Jane finds employment, or there are additional social security benefits that she could claim, this will not, of course, prevent other people in a similar situation to Jane from experiencing similar problems.

It is important that social workers are aware of how this interplay between material and emotional stresses may have their impact. Gould (2006), for example, shows how parents' experience of mental health problems can often be related to experiencing high levels of poverty, and charts the impact these factors have on parents' capacity to parent their children. Katz et al (2007) show how parents living in poverty face an array of issues that their more affluent counterparts do not. They recognise that research says little about the ways in which poor parents cope under these conditions, and therefore how 'good parenting' may mitigate the effects of poverty on children; nonetheless, as they observe, most parents possess strong coping skills in the face of such adversity. The approach mentioned earlier regarding Jane shows how social work has the potential to encourage and develop the strengths that she possesses. This requires an empowering approach by the social worker to assist her in addressing the emotional and material problems that she faces.

In discussing the principles of partnership, empowerment has explicitly been used as a means to enhance Jane's control over her situation. However, it is important to be clear what is actually meant by empowerment. For service users experiencing poverty, powerlessness is a crucial element in reinforcing feelings of hopelessness. To work in an empowering way requires social workers to enable access to appropriate resources, encouraging access to information and control over how resources are distributed and planned for. This means that service users define and control what issues they want to consider and the ways in which those issues will be addressed. It requires the full participation of those involved in the formulation, implementation and evaluation of decisions, determining the functioning and wellbeing of themselves and their wider social environment.

Empowerment

In working with service users in poverty the principles of empowerment require social workers to consider the personal power that they have in relation to service users. They should consider ways in which that power can be shared and transferred to service users. Empowerment is a concept for which there is no common agreement. Some observers highlight the primacy of individual empowerment while others, although not decrying such an approach, prioritise the collective and social aspects of empowerment (Adams, 2003). In terms of combating the problems of poverty that confront service users, both approaches are necessary. For example, the individual problems of a service user's relationship with Jobcentre Plus may be a unique experience for the service user, but may very well be experienced in similar ways by others in their contact with Jobcentre Plus.

In developing empowering practice the social worker is therefore required to enter into the world of the service user; this is akin to an empathetic approach, but goes beyond this by requiring the social worker to see the commonalities of one service user's experience with others. To understand poverty in this way connects an individual service user's experience with others that can move beyond the dangers of pathologising or blaming service users for their poverty by showing how others' experience may be similar.

In this regard, the service user's interpretation of events and problems in their life is therefore central. It is not the social worker's role to take the view of the expert but to validate the service user's consciousness of their situation. This counters those experiences by those living in poverty where their definitions of events are often invalidated by assumptions about a person's competence, knowledge and understanding of their own situation. As Krumer-Nevo and Benjamin (2008) argue, countering the narratives that stigmatise and discount the knowledge and competence of poor people's experience can be conceptualised as:

- *Developing a structural/contextual counter-narrative.* Fook (2012) argues in relation to AOP that contextualising service users' narratives enables an understanding that places their situation within a wider social context; identifying the structural causes of problems involved with poverty counters the blaming of service users as responsible for or causing the problems they find themselves in.
- *Empowering poor people to see they have power to affect their own situation.* By working in partnership with service users, listening to how they see their problems and encouraging them to work out their own strategies, as in the case study above, greater confidence and autonomy can be developed.
- *Enabling the voice of poor people to be heard as starting points for action.* The process of listening and recognising the particular ways in which service users living in poverty articulate their own problems and solutions to problems can enable

service users to develop positive action to counter their situation, either individually or collectively.

The analysis highlights the value of each of these counter-narratives in addressing the practical needs of people living in poverty, both at an individual and structural level. In considering the dynamics of empowerment, two aspects are important:

- control, so that people define their own situation and their needs within this;
- self-actualisation, enabling service users to take power for themselves through developing their confidence and self-esteem, their skills and knowledge.

Citizen approaches to empowerment

Crouch (2003) makes a distinction between consumerist/market approaches and citizenship/democratic approaches to empowerment. Service users who do not purchase services or who have little resources in order to do so would therefore not be able to directly effect change in influencing the agency. This is because in a consumerist model service users have a negative influence in that, as consumers of a service, they can withdraw from a service and seek an alternative. Many of the service users living in poverty do not have this choice.

Voice becomes the only way for people living in poverty to mount an effective challenge to agency policies. This requires social workers and service users using the existing structures of consultation, and also calling for new initiatives with the aim of acquiring greater influence over organisational change. It also requires social workers to work alongside service user organisations who advocate on behalf of their members; for example, many people with disabilities have organised themselves to oppose the WRA 2012 (such as Black Triangle at http://blacktrianglecampaign.org).

Empowerment and psychological impact

Anand and Lea (2011) suggest that using techniques of empowerment may not only enable service users to have a greater voice in and control over services that affect them, but may have positive effects in themselves. They highlight work undertaken in the health sector that suggests that through patients being actively involved and consulted in their treatment, positive effects can be measured in terms of health improvement. For example, where the clinical style was designed to motivate and encourage patients to make decisions jointly about their treatment, positive results were obtained. This leads Anand and Lea to suggest, although with some caution, that research methods and designs that can codify apparently philosophical and political economy concepts such as empowerment can be linked to hard outcome measures in terms of the increased positive functioning of individuals.

Advocacy

While the principles of empowerment and partnership may enable service users to develop their own competence and resilience in finding solutions to the problem of their poverty, there will be some occasions when social workers will have to advocate on behalf of service users. Much research has shown that when social workers advocate appropriately for service users, the outcomes can be more successful than if they had not done so (Wilks, 2012). In relation to advocacy around issues of poverty, service users' incomes can be significantly enhanced (Becker, 1997). Social workers advocating for a service user may face problems in having to work effectively under the rules of the social work bureaucracy that may impose, for example, time limits on working with service users. The policies of the organisation may also require that service users have to pay for their own services, or if the service is means tested, they may be unable to access a service free at the point of use. Service users may see differences in the kinds of services available to those living in poverty who receive a basic service and those service users willing and able to pay for more enhanced care. Social workers may then be faced with a conflict of interest, caught between advocating for a service user to access a service while the social work organisation that employs them may be rationing access to such a service. The social worker therefore has to be clear with the service user that there may be a cut-off point where a service user may be better accessing an independent advocate when the social workers organisation imposes time limits on further intervention. For example, the Fair Access to Care Services (FACS) criteria operated by all local authorities has narrowed the eligibility for care services or removed some groups from access to it. The ability of the social worker to advocate on behalf of a service user may therefore be constrained, requiring the social worker to encourage the service user to access an independent advocate or use the local political process (contact a local councillor, for example), if they feel the service user is unfairly being denied access to a service. However, this should only be contemplated when the social worker has exhausted all formal avenues within the organisation to advocate on behalf of the service user.

Minimal intervention

Minimal intervention in relation to AOP refers to the value of working with service users that seeks to use only the minimum of the formal legal power that social workers have authority to use. Power used by social workers can be positive as well as negative. The use of social workers' power to advocate and intervene at levels of organisations that have proved inaccessible for service users in poverty is one such positive example mentioned earlier. The intervention of social workers to protect service users from the illegitimate actions of others is another – this may be in terms of advocating on behalf of service users against the unscrupulous methods of credit companies that charge exorbitant levels of interest on loans. To avoid the disempowering of service users by inappropriate recourse to the use of formal powers, Payne (2000) highlights a three-stage approach:

• The primary level – the stage of initial contact and assessment.
• The secondary level – the stage at which the social worker and service user negotiate and develop their work together.
• The tertiary level – where more formal often statutory intervention may be required.

In terms of working with issues of poverty, there is much that can be achieved at the primary level. This involves assessing how services can be mobilised and adapted to offset the impact of poverty. Typically this may involve basic welfare rights work or looking at how services, for example, around family support, may help. It may also involve activating community resources so that individuals are less isolated and have access to a wider resource network. The secondary level involves identifying problems early, before they escalate into something more serious. This may be by intervening, as in the case of Jane, to provide support from the schools for her two children so that they do not experience the bullying and the exclusion that they have so far experienced. If Jane's situation has deteriorated, some kind of formal intervention is required at the tertiary level. Assuming that Jane experiences a complete emotional breakdown, whereby she may be in danger of requiring intervention from mental health services, the social worker should seek to reduce the consequences for Jane by encouraging her to seek help on a voluntary basis rather than being required to accept treatment, if this was deemed appropriate.

An example of where minimal intervention has become compromised is in the area of looked-after children. The government's latest figures of the numbers of looked-after children show that the overall number of children in care (76,050) has risen by 13 per cent since 2008. The number of looked-after children has increased steadily each year since 2008, and is now higher than at any point since 1997. The majority of looked-after children – 62 per cent in 2012 – are provided with a service due to abuse or neglect. These figures are worrying, but the most significant statistic shows that much of the increase in 2012 is accounted for by the rise in the number of children aged under one who started to be looked-after. In the year ending 31 March 2012, 5,880 children in this age group started to be looked-after. This represents an increase of 10 per cent from 2011. This shows that social workers are taking children into care in greater numbers and at an earlier age, which suggests that they are resorting to more formal procedures at an earlier stage in their intervention than in previous years (DfE, 2012). Why should this be the case? Research has not been conducted to date into the reasons for such an increase, but there has been a groundswell of opinion that has begun to put pressure on local authority social services departments for earlier intervention. Barnardo's, the children's charity, commissioned research by the think tank Demos (Hannon et al, 2010), which advocated earlier involvement, and the current

Minister for Education Michael Gove and the House of Commons Education Select Committee (2012) have all called for earlier intervention.

Critiquing anti-oppressive approaches to service users in poverty

In outlining anti-oppressive approaches to poverty, so far this chapter has not considered some of the pitfalls of working in such a way. AOP is not without its critics, and it is important to consider these criticisms as they may frustrate efforts at empowering service users. Sakamoto and Pitner (2005) argue that AOP social work is in danger of falling into what Freire (1997) called the teacher (social worker)–student (service user) trap. In this relationship the teacher is all-knowing and imparts knowledge to the student. If social workers automatically frame the problem for the service user in terms of oppression, they may well miss what the service user is trying to tell them about their particular needs. This becomes just another imposed discourse on service users rather than an open dialogue to discuss their needs.

To avoid such a situation, Sakamoto and Pitner (2005) argue that social workers need to reflect upon their own practice and review the assumptions they make about their role and their organisation, to see how they may be unwittingly reinforcing the oppression of service users. In addressing the organisation social workers need to understand how policies and procedures may act to suppress and deny the distribution of resources to alleviate service users' poverty (for example, the practice of giving loans to families in need under Section 17 of the Children Act 1989), even though such families may be living in dire poverty.

This leads us to the question as to who the expert is in relation to identifying need. Empowerment suggests that it is the service user. However, as Wilson and Beresford (2000) argue, there is a danger that the professionalisation of AOP becomes just another approach to practice which forms part of the social workers' toolkit where the service user is distanced and silenced, as AOP becomes a product of professional expertise.

In looking at social workers' response to poverty, Sakomoto and Pitner (2005) argue that we need to start from a sense of scepticism so that we do not assume that AOP, as it has developed in the past, has been any more effective than other approaches. In developing a more critical approach to AOP we might also have to face the discomfort of realising that AOP has, as some writers have argued, been co-opted by the state. McLaughlin (2005) suggests that AOP has become institutionalised and has, in effect, become just one more technique to control and police the behaviour of service users. Although some elements of McLaughlin's argument can be criticised (see Chapter 6), the extent to which AOP has been regarded as part of the institutional apparatus of the state can be considered by this observation:

> However, in the sense that it is about fostering individual personal change and enforcing a new moral consensus from above, the anti-oppressive social worker is well placed for personally policing, not politically empowering the disadvantaged. (McLaughlin, 2005, p 300)

Millar (2008) argues that AOP in the hands of some social workers has become a way of policing service users' language towards more politically acceptable terms while doing little to affect service users' material situation and addressing the problems that they feel should be addressed.

In addressing AOP in a way that can avoid the problems mentioned earlier, social workers need to be more self-critical in their approach to working with service users. In particular, they need to develop their own critical consciousness of their power, informally in their interaction with service users, so that their knowledge and expertise is shared with the service user and also so that the social worker appreciates the service user's knowledge of their own situation. Social workers also need to be aware of their formal power and the fear that service users living in poverty may have of social workers using such power in inappropriate ways.

Sakomoto and Pitner (2005) call this a process of critical consciousness, whereby the social worker is both reflective of their own power but also maintains a clear orientation towards achieving social justice for service users. This is an approach where psychology and sociology intersect. It requires social workers examining their formal power as social workers and also their own social location. For the UK this inevitably requires an understanding of their class position, their gender and racial positioning, although this is not exhaustive. For example, the majority of social workers are women who inevitably work with mostly women service users – how their class and racial positioning influences their response in terms of gender becomes crucial in this process of critical consciousness. Barn's work (2007), in relation to families and children from BME backgrounds, highlights the interplay of these different social divisions and the importance of social context in working effectively with this group of service users.

Service users recognise that issues of poverty, for example, in children and family work, are not sufficiently appreciated as real and enduring problems by social workers as, for example, parenting issues. There is often a disconnection between the two in some social workers' practice. This has been evidenced by the way in which volunteers working in family support tend to be valued over social workers, precisely because the majority of volunteers appreciate that parenting problems are often caused by poverty, particularly if they themselves have been the recipients of such help in the past (see Parrott et al, 2006; Gray, 2009).

As Sakomoto and Pitner (2005, p 442) identify:

> When social workers enter helping relationships, they enter with their own biases and prejudices. It is these biases and prejudices that can, and often do, affect how they listen to the problems of their service users and, ultimately, how they proceed to address them.

To develop a critical consciousness requires a recognition that however social workers might strive to be aware of class issues in poverty work, they must also be aware of the unwritten and often unexpressed ways in which they may unwittingly reinforce povertyism. To do this, social workers need to check out their practice with service users and continually reflect on how they engage with service users living in poverty. It is to work from the discomfort that they may not always eradicate bias in their work, but to recognise that this is a continual professional process of interrogating practice to enable social justice for service users; likewise, to interrogate the organisations social workers work for to see how they contribute or not towards social justice and to investigate how organisations may hold within them often unconscious assumptions about service users that are oppressive. To use the example of 'whiteness', many scholars have sought to investigate organisations to see how their operation may embed notions of white bias within their policies and procedures that may not be immediately visible (Williams and Parrott, 2012).

Of course social workers themselves occupy different privileged and unprivileged positions, thus understanding their social location and what privilege this brings is important, but it is also necessary to see in what ways social workers can be disadvantaged within their employing organisations. For example, the onset of managerialist approaches to social work has led to a significant limitation of social workers' ability to determine the content of their practice (Green, 2009). It is difficult to see how social workers can expect to empower others if they themselves are disempowered and allow this to continue within their work organisations. Social workers need to be able to find ways of countering those aspects of their employing organisations' policies and procedures that have oppressive consequences for their practice. This requires a more collective orientation through working with other social workers, administrators and support workers to determine how best to develop more control over their work. This therefore requires them to be a member of a trade union and a professional association, which will provide them with both a forum for discussing those issues that bear down on a social workers' ability to engage in an empowering way with service users and to campaign for better conditions and resources that will enable them to work more effectively. For example, in the UK many trade unions have been engaged in campaigns against low pay and better resourcing of public services that will have an immediate relevance for publicly employed social workers and also for service users.

Summary

This chapter has explored AOP in working with service users living in poverty. It has outlined an approach that reflects the values of AOP and used a case study to provide an example of how this approach can be developed. It has questioned existing approaches to AOP and has highlighted some of the criticisms that have been aimed at this way of working. In particular social workers who recognise the importance of language in describing the experience of those living in poverty must also address the material conditions which contribute to the lived reality of poverty. This requires an awareness of the ways in which their own organisations may contribute to service users lack of material resources but also the ways in which other agencies such as the Department for Work and Pensions may be implicated in this process. Social workers have to intervene sometimes to control aspects of service users conduct but this should not prevent them from addressing the material conditions which often constitute such behaviour. Finally, it has shown how a critical consciousness towards AOP can assist in developing more effective ways of working with service users who experience poverty.

Recommended reading

Ferguson, I. and Woodward, R. (2009) *Radical social work in practice: Making a difference*, Bristol: Policy Press.

Fook, J. (2012) *Social work: A critical approach to practice*, London: Sage Publications.

6

Social work organisations:
responding to poverty

In developing a more critical approach to AOP in relation to poverty it was argued in Chapter 5 that social workers needed to consider three key elements:

- the needs of the service user
- the nature of the social system
- the nature of the professional role.

This chapter looks at the organisation of social work within the wider social context of the UK, investigating how social work organisations can influence the levels of poverty service users experience. In the UK the majority of social workers (80 per cent) are employed by the state, therefore the way that the state organises the delivery of social work services has a significant impact on the quantity and quality of services provided.

Social workers in the UK are mostly employed within local authorities, and generally work in children and family departments or in adult service departments. In order for state social work to be effective, social workers have to follow specific policies, procedures and guidelines in order to administer the services they are responsible for. It is therefore the nature of the policies and procedures that can influence the success or otherwise of social workers' intervention with service users. In addition, the way that social workers interpret these policies can influence how well they respond to service users' needs.

The organisation of social work services has been influenced by two imperatives in recent years. The first is that of the market as a result of the NHS and Community Care Act 1990 – adult services have become increasingly delivered through the medium of the market. This legislation required local authorities to act as commissioners of services and to contract out services to the private and voluntary sectors. As a result, the contracting out of residential and domiciliary services has led to the total dominance of the private sector in the provision of such services. The White Paper, *Caring for our future* (DH, 2012), observes that 90 per cent of residential care provision and 80 per cent of domiciliary care provision is now run by the private sector. The White Paper also signals an expansion in the market for social care by the Developing Care Markets for Quality and Choice (DCMQC) programme that will assist local authorities in building their capacity to organise and deliver an expanded market for social care services. Indeed, the proposals envisage new duties placed on local authorities to shape market provision in their area.

Running parallel with the marketisation of social work has been the development of managerial systems, transferring the methods of private management into the public sector. The onset of managerial systems in social work has been well documented (see Harris and White, 2009, for an early assessment of this process). The introduction of managerial approaches has met much criticism – recent government-sponsored reports have talked of the baleful influence of bureaucratic managerial systems crowding out the social work role. *The Munro review* (2012) highlighted the difficulties and challenges contained within the current child protection system, finding that child protection practice was replete with procedures that reflected a bureaucratic rather than a professional focus. Munro described a culture of compliance where social workers were increasingly expected to follow procedures and guidance, leading to a level of prescription that inhibited their ability to exercise discretion and make informed professional judgements.

The convergence of market provision and bureaucratic management has provided a straitjacket into which social workers are struggling to respond sensitively to service users living in poverty.

For some critics, such as Bauman (1994), this configuration of an increasingly marketised delivery of service, underpinned by managerial control of social work and social care services, produces the worst of both worlds. It is a bureaucratised system that limits social workers' professional discretion within a configuration of services that are contracted out to the private sector where the concerns of cost-efficiency crowd out questions of effectiveness and wider ethical considerations.

Social work organisations and poverty

The Macpherson report (1999) highlighted how organisations may work in ways that (in this case, racially) discriminate against the very people they are meant to serve. Thus, for social workers to work in an effective way to counter poverty, they should have a clear idea as to what the positive and negative aspects of their organisations' policies are in combating it. Tronto (2010, p 158), for example, asks in relation to institutions and care:

> If we are committed to policies to improve care we need also to be able to answer the question: how can we tell which institutions provide good care?

She argues that the increased influence of the market in provision of care undermines standards of practice – as competition between providers may be useful to motivate providers into more cost-effective ways of providing care, it does not necessarily enable standards of care to be delivered. Competition, she suggests, focuses on the notion that one provider is better than another in terms of quantity rather than the quality of what is being provided. Indeed, some writers on the ethics of business are highly sceptical that business can operate from the value base required for social work. Bartlett and Preston (2000), for example, argue that a key problem in business is that organisations are profit-making mechanisms that have no interest in the good of society. Such organisations need to be convinced that a direct benefit will be achieved for them in order to act ethically.

If private business and the ethics that reflect business increasingly influence the delivery of care, there has to be a synergy between the pursuit of private interest and the public good. For those on the political right this synergy is possible and desirable; for those from the political left the dominance of market-based principles crowds out any public benefit in favour of the private interests of businesses and their shareholders.

The moral philosopher Sandel (2012) has argued vehemently that the use of markets, particularly in areas that require the delivery of such services as social work, undermine altruistic behaviour and corrupt relevant ethical issues such as respect and autonomy. In social work the practical engagement with ethical issues is a constant feature of the interaction between social workers and service users. An example of market-like approaches compromising the ethics of social work can be seen in the 'marketing' of children for adoption. Higgins and Smith (2002) outline how children are marketed as commodities to be consumed by prospective adopters as they peruse the pictures of children being offered for adoption through advertising children in newspapers and television.

Similar questions remain in respect to the development of managerialism. Rogowski (2011) argues that there are two factors that have contributed to the managerialisation of social work. First, with the incremental rise of policies and procedures across all aspects of social work in response to media criticism and government concern, social workers are subject to increased scrutiny and supervision of their practice. The needs of service users become engulfed with how the organisation delivers service outcomes in relation to, for example, how cost-effectiveness has been achieved. In order to achieve these outcomes the practice of social workers has to be managed in terms of the time they spend with service users and the way social workers make decisions about their practice. In terms of allocating resources, resource panels have proliferated in social work, where managers monitor the recommendations of social workers to access resources on behalf of service users in order to control costs. Second, managers who may have been practising social workers themselves have either been co-opted into this managerial discourse or have been brought in from the business world to achieve the desired outcomes. This in turn focuses managers' commitments and interests to that of the organisation and its smooth functioning for itself rather than a focus on the practice of social work and the needs of service users. As Rogowski (2011, p 163) points out in relation to some managers' lack of social work qualifications:

> The obvious example of this is that following the demise of Social Services Departments, many of the subsequent heads or senior managers of the subsequent adults and children's services did not have any experience of social work, though they might be qualified in or

have experience of business. Following the Baby Peter tragedy, the lack of social work experience by many senior managers was one of the many criticisms of London Borough of Haringey's Children's Services.

Given the discussion mentioned earlier concerning the way in which social work organisations have reoriented themselves towards the market and managerialism, it is important to see how these changes have influenced social workers' practice in working with service users in poverty. Two elements of this are considered: first, the expansion of markets across social work and social care and the use of means testing service users for services; and second, the application of rationing techniques and the procedures used to limit the extent of social workers' discretion. In relation to the first point any use of charging and means testing of services is likely to have a significant impact on service users' access to services and on their levels of income. With regards to the second point, the use of procedures to contain the professional discretion of social workers has the potential to limit social workers' creativity and professional engagement with service users in finding solutions to the poverty that they experience.

Markets and social care

In considering how service users access care services and the consequences this may have for the provision of services, it is important to consider the system for assessing the needs of service users who require social care. The local authority has a duty under the NHS and Community Care Act 1990 (Section 47) to assess a person's care needs. After the assessment is completed a decision is made as to what kind of service is required. The decision to provide a service is determined by the local authority's eligibility criteria that should reflect national guidance, and is commonly known as FACS.

The guidance was reviewed in 2010, and subsequently 'Prioritising need in the context of *Putting People First*: A whole system approach to eligibility for social care' became the benchmark for local authorities. The guidance sets out a framework for identifying people's social care needs that are placed into four bands. Once an individual has been assessed, the local authority decides where a person's needs fit into the bands, which are: critical, substantial, moderate and low.

All local authorities use this system, but they have discretion to set their threshold individually within the bands, based on an assessment of their resources, local expectations and costs. Local authorities therefore have a great deal of freedom in setting their threshold, and given the relative demand on resources within an authority, it is likely that those authorities with relatively less resources and higher demands placed on them are likely to set their threshold higher. This results in considerable variation between local authorities where one authority may set their threshold at 'critical' while another may set theirs at 'substantial', leading to variability of access to services depending on where the service user lives.

Since 2007 local authorities have been operating under increasing financial pressures that have resulted in many local authorities tightening their eligibility criteria. Most authorities now only provide publicly funded care to people with critical or substantial needs:

> Prior to 2006, only half the local authorities in England set their eligibility levels at "critical" or "substantial", whereas in 2011 4% will only fund care for people with "critical" needs and a further 78% set eligibility at "substantial" needs. (EHRC, 2011, p 18)

The result of such stringency is that more service users have to pay for their own home care or go without the support they require. The differences between a person with moderate and substantial needs is often one of professional judgement, which means that social workers who wish to maintain service users' incomes may need to use their discretion appropriately to enable them to access care supported by public funds.

The way that local authorities take referrals for community care assessments is beginning to change. Often the first point of contact may be through telecare, as local authorities streamline their point of contact. Much information about access to services is also provided online. which can be problematic for many service users, and particularly for older people. Six million people aged 65 and over have never used the internet. Breaking this down by age cohort, 42 per cent of those aged 65-74 and 76 per cent of those aged 75 and over have never used the internet (ONS, 2011). Coleman and Harris (2008) argue that the expansion of telecare will do nothing to enable service users to access services more effectively, and suggest that greater research is needed to analyse its consequences for service users, to avoid exclusion via the internet. Those older people who lack the resources to access this technology are likely to be particularly excluded. In addition, the uses of such technological systems curtail social workers' ability to fully assess enquiries that service users may make for assistance.

Figures accessed from The Poverty Site (2012) highlight the problems for people living in poverty if access to services becomes increasingly dependent on access via the internet:

- Although the proportions have fallen substantially over the last decade, more than half of households in the poorest fifth still lack a PC, as do a fifth of households on average incomes. Internet access at home follows a similar pattern: 60% of households in the poorest fifth lack such access, as do 30% of households on average incomes. In other words, lack of Internet access is twice as common in the poorest fifth compared with those on average incomes.
- In addition to income, age is clearly also a factor affecting Internet access: whilst "only" 20% of households where the head of the household is aged under 50 lack such access, this rises to 75%

> for those aged 70 and over. Combining income and age: the vast
> majority (85%) of households aged 70 and over in the poorest fifth
> lack Internet access. (The Poverty Site, 2012)

The Equalities and Human Rights Commission (EHRC, 2011) have raised concerns that older people in real need may be denied a service. In relation to contact by telephone, older people with cognitive or hearing impairments may find such points of contact difficult to access, thus potentially leaving an older person without access to an assessment. In addition, the introduction of computer-based self-assessment, used mostly for personalised support, is also inaccessible to many older people, and this may lead to low take-up of services. As discussed previously, many people living in poverty become used to merely surviving and therefore underestimate their needs (see Chapter 5). In respect to older people and low take-up of social work services, McDonald (2010) provides many examples of the problems confronting social work services if they are to enable older people to access services effectively, particularly in relation to direct payments.

The EHRC (2011) reported that they interviewed a director of a voluntary organisation who observed that some local authorities use the telephone interview as a screening process. Thus older people would be passed on to a voluntary organisation if the person outlined 'needed a bit of help around the home' rather than seeing this as an opportunity to explore the service user's needs in full.

Age UK was concerned, as part of their evidence to the EHRC, that central telephone points for access to all services presents barriers to older people, as telephone screening is likely to overlook significant aspects of a person's difficulties that they may be experiencing. This is significant, as older people tend to be reticent about disclosing their need for personal care. Local authorities are required to provide an assessment even where they may not currently provide a service, or where an older person would have to meet all the costs of their care.

Assuming that the service user receives a thorough assessment and that their identified needs meet the eligibility criteria, that person is deemed to have 'eligible needs'. The local authority has a legal duty to provide a service or arrange suitable services to meet the needs identified.

Once the level of need has been determined, service users are subject to a financial assessment to determine how much they should pay towards the cost of the services; this assessment is based on a person's level of financial resources, resulting in a means test. Once charges have been set as a result of the assessment of a person's income, government guidance expects that a person's income should not fall below a specified level. After paying any charge for a home care service, a person's income should not fall below the basic level of Income Support (personal allowance plus any premiums) plus an additional 25 per cent of this amount. In essence, the operation of this means-tested system reduces people's income to one of poverty, given our analysis in Chapter 3. Social workers involved in these assessments need to ensure that if charges leave a service user below these figures, the charges should be reviewed. However, if the service user receives meals as part of the package, these are charged at a set rate, and the person will be expected to pay as they are outside the calculation of the charge (Age UK, 2012).

The regulations and procedures governing the access and delivery of home care are highly complex and not easily understandable, even to the professionals involved. Complexity results in greater confusion for service users and professionals, that in turn can lead to a vital service for impoverished service users being wrongly assessed and/or denied. Given the way people living in poverty experience stigma by being required to have their income and savings investigated, it becomes a mark of shame for many when they are deemed to be requiring the assessed service as a result of their lack of individual income. This sense of stigma is further reinforced as older people's experience of social work and social care services is that they are often seen as passive, lacking independence and requiring healthcare rather than wider social support and enablement (Bowers et al, 2009). Older people living in poverty face dual discrimination through this process in that they are discriminated against on the grounds of age while receiving a basic service if they are unable to purchase additional services on top of those that have been assessed.

The minimising of older people's needs was identified by the Centre for Policy on Ageing (2008) that conducted a literature review for the Department of Health into discrimination against older people. They found that there were different cost ceilings applied to care packages for older people than to younger adults with disabilities, resulting in a lower capacity to meet a range of needs. This restricted older people's options, particularly in developing valued social aspects of daily living. The use of cost ceilings in relation to older people operated so that if the cost of going into residential care was a cheaper option than supporting someone at home, then older people were more likely to enter residential care at an earlier point than younger disabled adults. Of course those older people with additional income could remain in the community, all things being equal, for a longer period than those living in poverty. The dual impact of ageism and poverty is also felt in the benefits system where a differential access to funds is afforded to younger adults, enabling them to use such universal allowances as Attendance Allowance to fund more flexible ways to provide support in the community.

Finally, a means-tested system that charges for care acts as a barrier for service users in taking up services. The Coalition on Charging (2008) undertook an extensive survey with service users of all ages using home care. They found that 80 per cent of the people interviewed no longer using care services said that charging had played a part in their decision to end use of the services. They also questioned the nature of the financial assessment that was deemed inadequate, as only 29 per cent felt that their essential expenditure as a result of their impairment/health condition had been adequately taken into account. Some 23 per cent believed that only some of their essential costs were considered. As a result, this had an important impact on people's lives. Where essential costs were not being accounted for then this increased the level of spending on such items, thus reducing people's ability to pay for leisure and social activities. Charges for 60 per cent of respondents had risen more than inflation, thus impoverishing those on benefits whose incomes from benefit is upgraded in line with inflation. This is likely to be even more problematic now that increases in benefits have been pegged to 1 per cent of inflation, as of 2013. These findings also echoed the organisations consulted: 58 per cent of organisations surveyed strongly argued that the current financial assessments did not adequately account for people's essential expenditure. Some of the examples given, where expenditure was not accounted for, were heating when the temperature needed to be kept at a constant level, laundry in the case of incontinence, and essential dietary requirements relating to a person's impairment. Service users experienced difficulties in affording all the support they needed – 54 per cent said they either could not afford the support, or only with difficulty. In general, having to cut back on spending elsewhere in a service user's budget meant going out less to socialise, and not being able to afford transport. More personal costs included having to stop having their hair washed and cut, cutting down on heating and lighting and not being able to buy family and friends Christmas and birthday presents. These findings also correlate with the Counsel and Care (2008) survey of charging in local authorities that found fewer older people receiving services and experiencing rising costs for their care. Local authorities are providing increased services for a smaller band of service users while little or no help is being provided for those identified as having low levels of need.

This, in turn, has a domino effect on friends and relatives. One in five carers have given up work or been unable to take up work as a result of care responsibilities (Coalition on Charging, 2008); this often leads to problems of ill health for carers. It was estimated that around 200,000 carers claimed the old Incapacity Benefit when the survey was completed in 2008.

Many local authorities do try and maintain some low level support, but this is often provided outside of the local authority and is supported by grant aid, which is becoming increasingly rationed as local authorities face significant cuts to their budgets. However, as Clough et al (2007) found, many authorities did fund support services such as befriending schemes, advocacy and low-level domiciliary care. The key problem in developing such services was lack of funding and the related problem of block contracts. Block contracts are made for a defined-level service bought for a specified price. They are cheaper to operate and cheaper to buy in, but they are not flexible, and reflect traditional forms of service such as day care and meals on wheels. By comparison, more expensive spot contracts that are specific arrangements designed to fit around an individual's needs are rarely made available.

Markets and residential care

The majority of residential care beds are now found within the private residential sector and some £4 billion is spent on funding residential care. The private sector has experienced a number of problems in recent years in relation to funding; for example, the Southern Cross Group was unable to maintain its homes and had to sell them on to a private equity company (Scourfield, 2011). Criticism from the sector has often pointed to the inadequate levels of funding provided by government, leaving individuals' families to supplement the care costs of their family member where they can.

Private care homes may be funded from three sources:

- self-funding residents
- third party 'top-up' arrangements
- local authorities.

The effect of poor levels of funding means that care homes struggle to provide even adequate care, but as we have seen in relation to home care, self-funders and relatives (via third party top-ups) end up subsidising the shortfall in local authority funding. As Scourfield (2007) argues, this problem applies to the local authority and voluntary sector and is likely to get worse in the context of the Coalition government's deficit reduction measures. The private sector has also been admonished for its poor quality of care compared to local authorities and the voluntary sector, with the Care Quality Commission (CQC) reporting:

> The quality of privately run care services is generally lower than those run by councils or voluntary organisations, although the costs were often lower as well. (2011a, p 58)

The consequences of poor quality care in the residential care sector means that those who can afford to choose which care home they reside in are able to access better quality homes. Studies of people living in residential care show that people from poorer backgrounds are more likely to become residents than those with greater financial resources. Indeed, those service users who have little or no saved income are therefore likely to be provided with residential care that meets minimum standards, and will have less choice in determining the care home in which they would prefer to reside (Wilton, 2003; Young et al, 2006).

The Children Act 2004: policy, procedure and poverty

This section focuses on the implications of the increased introduction of policies and procedures in relation to social work with children and families. The basis for current practice in regard to working with children and families can be found in the Green Paper, *Every Child Matters* (2004) and the subsequent Children Act 2004, which were largely a response to concerns expressed in the Laming report regarding Victoria Climbié (2003). *Every Child Matters* (2004) reflected an attempt to create a universal approach to providing support for children and families. It proposed a broad system of intervention that sought to identify children with particular problems at an early stage in their lives. The intention was to integrate a number of measures that would work towards ending child poverty and to encourage the potential of every child. The subsequent Children Act 2004, in refining the policy and procedure for the assessment of children's needs, modified the Framework for the Assessment of Children in Need and their Families (2000) (which became the Common Assessment Framework, CAF), this came into operation in 2006. The intention of this modification was to move away from a narrow focus on child protection and the marginalising of socio–economic factors such as poverty within the assessment (Horvath, 2011).

The goal was to create a universal framework of services for children through a multidisciplinary approach in which a range of agencies would be drawn together to provide a more integrated community-focused response to children and their families. Unfortunately, within the context of the funding of adequate children's services, this policy would not attract any extra resources but was aimed at reframing and restructuring the existing palate of services.

The policy focused work with children around their educational needs, where the school became the hub around which the integration of services revolved. In the context of successive governments' approaches to combat poverty, education is seen as the means to employability in which paid work is the route out of poverty. From an organisational perspective this reorganisation around education resulted in the location of a Ministry for Children in the Department for Education that also attracted other responsibilities in relation to family support (for example, Sure Start moving from the domain of the Home Office). As Williams (2004, p 414) argued:

> Education as the basis to employability, and employability as the insurance against poverty is, then, a strong leitmotiv in the Green Paper.

The development of measures to integrate children's services and to fight poverty must also be understood within the previous Labour government's policy initiative to end child poverty. In 1999 the Labour government announced its commitment to end child poverty by 2020. Interim targets were set that envisaged child poverty declining by a quarter by 2004 and by a half by 2010. These targets have not been met, although the child poverty initiative has been partially successful, with child poverty declining by just over a quarter in 12 years rather than by a half, which was previously envisaged (Brewer et al, 2011). Before the end of the Labour government's time in office it had enacted the Child Poverty Act 2010. The legislation set out specific strategies to be undertaken to eradicate child poverty. In setting out the strategies there is much that echoes with the *Every Child Matters* agenda:

a) Promotion and facilitation of the employment of parents or of the development of the skills of parents.
b) Provision of financial support for children and parents.
c) Provision of information, advice and assistance to parents and the promotion of parenting skills.

d) Development of physical and mental health, education, childcare and social services.

e) A focus on housing, the built or natural environment and the promotion of social inclusion.

The Act places a duty on the Secretary of State to meet four targets on child poverty by 2020, covering:

- relative low income
- combined low income and material deprivation
- absolute low income
- persistent poverty.

It also required the government to set up a Poverty Commission to provide advice and guidance on how to develop a strategy for the elimination of child poverty. The Coalition government initially failed to constitute such a body, and in fact included a target of its own, the persistent poverty target. This target is rather vague as it has not been defined; nor is there any specific target set in place to be met by 2020. This subsequently led to a judicial challenge mounted by CPAG as the current government was required by the Act to produce a strategy after consulting with the Child Poverty Commission (which it had not set up at the time). The High Court agreed that the government should have consulted and taken advice from a child poverty commission and consulted on the inclusion of their persistent poverty criteria which, CPAG argued, was flawed. Essentially these criteria focused on a small number of families' behaviour (such as parents with drug or alcohol problems) as a contributing factor to poverty, yet these groups with such behavioural problems account for a relatively small number of families living in poverty. The current Coalition government has also set up a commission into child poverty but it has a broadened remit and as such may further dilute the original focus on poverty, as the body is now called the Child Poverty and Social Mobility Commission. It is the Coalition's position that social mobility, as defined through accessing work, is the best route out of poverty. This is questionable given the arguments explored in Chapter 3, particularly in relation to the numbers of people living in poverty who work. In addition, any advice that the new commission gives must take into account:

- economic circumstances, particularly the likely impact of any measure on the economy;
- fiscal circumstances, particularly the likely impact of any measure on taxation, public spending and borrowing.

Given the current economic climate and a government focus on cuts in public spending, the future for any further gains in the eradication of child poverty looks bleak. Brewer et al (2011) calculated that:

- The direct impact of the current government's announced reforms to personal tax and benefit policy will be to increase relative poverty among children by 200,000 in both 2015/16 and 2020/21, and among working-age adults by 200,000 and 400,000 in 2015/16 and 2020/21 respectively.
- Universal Credit should reduce poverty substantially, but the poverty-increasing effect of other government changes to personal taxes and state benefits will more than offset this.

In addition, Brewer et al (2011) calculate that both relative and absolute poverty for children and adults will rise substantially by 2021:

- The number of children in relative poverty is forecast to rise from 2.6 million in 2009/10 to 2.9 million in 2015/16 and 3.3 million by 2020/21 (measuring income before housing costs), and that of working-age adults from 5.7 million in 2009/10 to 6.5 million in 2015/16 and 7.5 million by 2020/21.
- Relative child poverty will rise from 20 per cent currently to 24 per cent by 2020/21, the highest rate since 1999/2000 and considerably higher than the 10 per cent target in the Child Poverty Act 2010.
- The proportion of children in absolute poverty (using the 2010/11 poverty line fixed in real terms) is forecast to rise to 23 per cent by 2020/21, compared with the 5 per cent target.
- Absolute poverty will rise considerably in the next few years as earnings growth is forecast to be weak but inflation high. Real median household income will remain below its 2009/10 level in 2015/16.

The Coalition government's approach to child poverty was set out in *A new approach to child poverty: Tackling the causes of disadvantage and transforming families' lives* (DWP, 2011). In the foreword Iain Duncan Smith, Minister for Work and Pensions, outlined the government's approach, which linked the issue of social mobility with poverty, as the quotation below identifies:

> This is a strategy founded on the understanding that poverty is about far more than income. The previous Government attempted to hit poverty targets by paying out more and more in welfare payments so as expenditure grew poverty for working-age adults increased and mobility failed to improve. Vast sums of cash were spent but the rungs on the ladder to prosperity didn't move any closer together. Previous Ministers announced they had made progress on child poverty but actually for too many their life chances did not alter. This is because the causal problems were never addressed. (DWP, 2011, p 2)

In signalling the change in policy it outlines a more targeted approach, focusing on what are described as the most disadvantaged families. This approach emphasises employment (as did the previous Labour government) as the route for parents out of poverty. In addition it valorises the behavioural changes assumed to follow from this as children 'benefit from a positive role model, a healthier and happier family, and a more stable home life' (DWP, 2011, p 4.). The Coalition therefore wishes to move away from targets based on income towards what they call 'life chances indicators'. In doing so the focus remains on improving education outcomes for children, developing earlier intervention where required, including physical and mental health support in the lives of families identified as problematic. It also identifies what they consider to be the most disadvantaged groups, such as:

• looked–after children
• children from some ethnic groups
• children with special educational needs
• teenage parents.

In targeting what are considered to be priority groups, the Coalition government has, as a result of the recent riots in 2011, focused on a group of 120,000 families as part of its Social Justice Strategy (DWP, 2012b). This group of families have been readily singled out as constituting a challenge to society requiring special treatment.

The government estimates that these families cost £9 billion through the involvement of different state services in responding to their chaotic 'lives'. These figures, as Levinas (2012) points out, are taken from the Department for Communities and Local Government (DCLG) website and are highly problematic in that the policies derived from the research do not follow from the research itself. The original research came from work that the now defunct Social Exclusion Unit carried out (Social Exclusion Task Force, 2007). Their analysis showed that in 2004 approximately 2 per cent of families had five or more of seven characteristics, which meant they were severely disadvantaged:

• no parent in the family is in work
• family lives in overcrowded housing
• no parent has any qualifications
• mother has mental health problems
• at least one parent has a long-standing limiting illness, disability or infirmity
• family has low income (below 60 per cent of median income)
• family cannot afford a number of food and clothing items.

As Levinas (2012) observes, these figures reflected an estimate of 117,000 families in England but were statistically questionable because they ignored errors in sampling and bias in that the poorest sections of society tend to have lower response rates. This means that the actual figures could be as high as 300,000 families; the figures themselves are also eight years out of date.

Given the feelings of stigma and isolation that families living in poverty experience, this particular policy response may further reinforce these negative attributes within people living in poverty but also encourage fear from the wider population. It is one thing to focus on research that identifies multiple disadvantage experienced by families; it is another to label such families 'families from hell' (as David Cameron has done; see Chapter 2), with little or no evidence to support such an assertion. The extent to which this group of families has become further stigmatised can be seen by the appointment of Louise Casey to lead the Troubled Families Unit who has called for tough action to control families:

> 'Yes, we have to help these families. But I also don't think we should soft-touch those families. We are not running some cuddly social workers' programme to wrap everybody in cotton wool.' (quoted in *Daily Telegraph*, 2012b)

Under the scheme to work with 'troubled families', each family has a dedicated worker to work intensively with them:

> Family Intervention Projects provide intensive, practical support to whole families. Each family is assigned a dedicated worker who assesses the family's needs, provides intensive one to one support until the most critical problems have been addressed and brings in and co-ordinates the support provided by other local agencies. They use a combination of support and sanction to motivate the family to change their behaviour. They use persistence and assertiveness with families to keep them engaged and following agreed steps. (DCLG, 2012, p 7)

This approach is similar to one that the previous Labour government developed, that is, Intensive Family Support Projects (see Nixon et al, 2006; National Centre for Social Research, 2010). This project, delivered by National Children's Homes, housed families in core accommodation where their behaviour was monitored and controlled, and as one respondent observed:

> 'I mean from day one it was like ... god, it was like a prison, you know what I mean? But I'm used to it now, sort of thing I don't go anywhere.' (Nixon et al, 2006, p 51)

As Garrett (2009) argues, there are a number of unexplored issues in relation to these projects and those currently being developed; in particular, the recipients of such interventions are overwhelmingly poor white women who often have significant mental and physical health problems.

Having questioned the statistical basis on which the government is basing its policy, subsequent criticism has also been made about the ethical standards used in the 'research' carried out by Louise Casey. Bailey (2012) contacted the DCLG as he was concerned that the families interviewed by Casey had not given their consent to be interviewed as part of the research. In reply, the DCLG considered that the interviews were not formal research as such, but 'dipstick/informal information gathering' (Bailey, 2012). As Bailey sardonically observed:

> If the report was not proper "social research", this would raise a whole new set of questions about why it was given such extensive press and media prominence and why it was considered a reliable basis for policy. How many other "dipstick" exercises have been given such coverage? Is it Government policy to move from "evidence-based policy" to "policy by dipstick"?

This episode is also redolent of the lack of respect afforded to such families that they can be interviewed in such a way. How far were these families giving free and informed consent? As Bailey (2012) argues, children and vulnerable adults have to be treated with care, particularly as one of the respondents was described as having learning difficulties and attention deficit hyperactivity disorder (ADHD); nothing suggests that these considerations were taken into account. Likewise, where personal data was collected in this report, ethical approval should have been sought. The confidentiality of these families' has also been compromised as many of the families are large, and details of family composition have been provided in the report; although the names of families have been changed, the details have not.

Many social workers working with families living in poverty would, as a matter of ethical professional practice, ensure as far as possible that service users give free and informed consent to any intervention that they may enter into voluntarily, and would also seek to maintain a service user's confidentiality at all times. This is not about wrapping people in 'cotton wool', but ensuring people's rights are respected. It would seem that the overarching discourse from the Coalition government and some sections of the media revolves around the blaming of such families for their position in society and in turn the use of shame as a means to discredit their motives for change. The construction of such a view of service users living in the most extreme forms of poverty seems more akin to Victorian conceptions of the 'residuum'. This is also in contrast to research that has emanated from the Intensive Family Support Projects by the National Centre for Social Research (2010), demonstrating the real efforts made by these families to improve their situation despite the many obstacles that they face.

Social work and family support

The measures put in place by the previous Labour government reflected a concern to provide services that attempted to deal with family poverty and the related stresses they experienced. In so doing it signalled that the state should take responsibility for children in society alongside parents, and reflects the notion of a social investment state whereby the state invests in children as a means of ensuring the future stability of society (Frost and Parton, 2009). In developing family support, agencies that have been charged with the responsibility have operated relatively independent of the local authority yet are tied into the range of services coordinated around children and families, usually through the role of the social worker. Agencies such as Sure Start and children's centres represent the contracting out of support services for children and parents in a similar way to that which operates in the adult sector. Likewise, social work with children and families has become more focused on a smaller section of this group as social work priorities have shifted from child support to child protection (Frost and Parton, 2009). The House of Commons Education Select Committee (2012) commented on the way thresholds triggering intervention with families were being set by local authorities. They took evidence suggesting a wide variation in the thresholds set. Where thresholds were set too low, social work services were being overwhelmed with large numbers of referrals, while setting thresholds too high resulted in children failing to receive the help they needed. There was much anecdotal evidence they received that suggested that financial stringency, leading to staff shortages and cutbacks in services, was leading to thresholds being set high. This is also reflected in adult social care, where it was observed that there was hard evidence for the increasing difficulty adults had in accessing care services.

In terms of combating the effects of poverty, the social work response has narrowed and is now entwined with child protection. Families who would have previously worked with social workers are now left to their own devices or are picked up through the CAF where their needs may be assessed as at a lower level, and they may be referred on for lower level support.

Local authorities have a duty under Section 17 of the Children Act 1989:

- to safeguard and promote the welfare of children in their area;
- as far as is consistent with that duty, promote the upbringing of children by their families, by providing a range of services appropriate to those children's needs.

A child is deemed to be in need of such intervention if they are:

- unable to achieve or maintain a reasonable standard of health or development without the provision of such services

or

- their health and development is significantly impaired without the provision of such services

or

- he/she has a disability.

However, social work services have not reached all of these children as the thresholds that operate to trigger intervention by social workers have been raised if there is no significant risk or evidence of harm. Research at the turn of the century showed that many referrals were dealt with within short time periods, often within 24 hours, and that in many instances no service was offered (DfES, 2002). More recent research illuminates this trend, showing that in many cases initial assessments are not thorough enough to pick up underlying needs (Horvath, 2011). Social workers therefore find themselves working under time pressure to meet initial assessment targets and increasingly, if not exclusively, with more serious child protection cases. For the local authority child protection is the overriding priority, so that work that can target the poverty experienced by such families is further downgraded. In particular, the exponential rise in policies and procedures governing social work intervention with families and children therefore limits social workers' use of professional judgement to work in ways other than what policy dictates. The need to complete initial assessments leads to both social workers and their managers working towards meeting time limits for assessment rather than focusing on the quality of the assessment itself. Broadhurst et al (2009) found that the initial assessment timescales were so limiting that workers took shortcuts, in order to 'sign off' the assessment within the timeframe. For example, although social workers are required to 'see the child' as part of the assessment, this contact was often desultory, while in relation to gathering information from parents, social workers gathered just enough to satisfy their supervising manager. Thus the space to make a significant interaction and to work with children and parents is circumscribed by the timeframe of the initial assessment, and therefore issues that may be significant in identifying problems of low income and poverty are likely to be overlooked or merely seen as 'normal' within families' experiences.

White et al's research (2009) into the CAF explored how practitioners interact with the CAF and the demands it places on them. The research took place across four local authorities between 2005 and 2006. The researchers observed practice and conducted focus groups and interviews with practitioners. A total of 280 CAFS were analysed. Participants expressed concern regarding the layout of the new form; it forced the practitioner to fragment aspects of the child's story that could lead to the information being drawn out of context. Workers displayed irritation at the fact that forms had character limits. However, some practitioners were still working with the handwritten forms, and there was evidence here of practitioners working around the form, such as writing outside of the boxes. However, the worker's discretion was limited as they had to produce the assessment in a standardised way. Many thought that the quality of the assessment was affected as a result. The design of the form meant that word limits on the enabled forms added further constraints, although the social workers were still able to exercise some discretion in finding ways to work around the form, as discussed above. Nevertheless, the framing of the CAF to enable it to be digitised placed significant limitations on the quality of the information provided, often missing significant contextual information, that is, social context in relation to a service user's situation.

The nature of this problem has been well documented and relates to the specific system used, that is, the Integrated Children's System. Ince and Griffiths (2010) argue that the system is taken from an industrial model that has been successful in terms of application to stock control, product marketing and customer relationship management, but it is less successful when dealing with broad contextual factors resulting, for example, in difficulties in documenting a chronology of events in relation to service users. In effect, due to its industrial origins, the system encourages a production line mentality of assessment rather than promoting a reflective process whereby information can be used to capture both a service user's narrative and the social context within which the narrative sits. A quote from Wastell et al (2009, p 263) outlines the difficulties in managing such a system:

> I used to tell my social workers to get the work with the family right, and then recording lags behind ... but I've been told I've got to stop that. So, I've had to say, cut your visits down, keep to 45 minutes and don't write so much. We've always resisted but we've come to the point where we've got to compromise practice, to devalue it because of the fear of spot inspection.

Service users value the intervention of social workers when they can spend time to listen to them. Gaining the trust of service users so that they feel comfortable in discussing aspects of their background and to identify their needs requires a greater investment of time than what the initial assessment process allows.

Discretion and professional social work

The extent to which social workers can negotiate more time and space to engage with service users living in poverty can be linked to the extent to which social workers feel constrained by their managers and the control exercised over them. This section identifies that the discretion that social workers may employ is a product of negotiation within their employing organisations. It is not the argument of this section to assume that social work discretion is of itself necessarily a 'good thing'. However, given the analysis of the policy and procedure mentioned earlier, it is also clear that social workers are not given the space, particularly at the initial assessment stage, to use their professional judgement to work in a positive, that is, anti-oppressive, way with service users.

The extent to which social workers can use their discretion has been understood through Lipsky's concept of the 'street-level bureaucrat'. Lipsky describes street-level bureaucrats as those who 'Interact directly with citizens in the course of their jobs, and who have substantial discretion in the execution of their work' (Lipsky, 1980, p 32). Lipsky identifies three factors that shape street-level bureaucrats' experience of discretion: the degree of freedom afforded them from the agency that is necessary to do the job, the practical requirement for street-level bureaucrats to make their own decisions due to the nebulous nature of policy and the ability of street-level bureaucrats to subvert policy (Evans and Harris, 2004, p 846). Professionals such as social workers must always make sense of the policy directives and guidelines in their interaction with service users. There is a constant tension between what those who control the policy intend to happen, and how the social worker interprets these guidelines in the light of actual experience on the ground. So for social workers working to alleviate the poverty of service users, there is always some space to use their street-level knowledge to interpret policies such as FACS in a way that can potentially transcend the strictures of the policy.

The capacity for social workers to exercise their discretion is contested within the literature. However, Ellis (2007), who studied social workers' role in the provision of direct payments to service users, argues that social workers still exercise considerable freedom in their practice. But for Ellis, the level of discretion used was exercised in a negative way. Access to direct payments was restricted by social workers making decisions as to who was able and appropriate to use them; this was significant in relation to older people who were understood and therefore assessed as not wanting to bother with such a procedure. In addition to making judgements about the appropriateness of some service users to make use of direct payments, social workers saw direct payments as a challenge to their role. They interpreted their role as being in control of access to services, and so were reluctant to enable service users' access to direct payments, seeing them as a subversion of their role. In particular, Ellis's research outlined how social workers rationed access to direct payments, seeing them as an illegitimate use of resources and/or seeing them as replacing valued existing services.

Evans (2011) also identified a considerable level of discretion operating at the local level, making a distinction between strategic management through the attempted enforcement of policy and procedure and the local level where practitioners and local managers (mostly social work practitioners themselves) were able to exercise considerable discretion. In relation to an older persons team, where the FACS eligibility criteria had tightened from level 3 to level 2, evidence showed that the practitioners largely moved service users from level 3 to 2. Admittedly this led to the strategic managers instituting resource panels that delayed access to services and also created a waiting list. However, at least in the case of those service users placed on a waiting list, they were actually given access to the particular resource rather than being denied it altogether. Both Evans and Ellis show that there is a continuing conflict between the strategic policy concerns to limit resources in Evans' case, or to institute direct payments in Ellis's case and social workers' discretion. Practitioners' response in trying to subvert the FACS criteria or limit the take-up of direct payments shows that control over practitioners' discretion is not all-embracing but more contingent. In this regard, social workers' levels of discretion can be utilised for more positive outcomes in relation to working with people living in poverty. This hinges around how social workers interpret the different policies and procedures, particularly around those areas that require social workers to assess service users and then identify if they fit criteria for resources and services.

Summary

This chapter has described the way social work organisations operate to enable or hinder social workers' engagement with poverty. It is the contention of this chapter that social work organisations in the UK have been increasingly shaped by the politics of neo-liberalism, with its emphasis on the rational management of markets to deliver social work outcomes. As Rothstein (1998) argues, organisations and institutions are not just empirical entities but also normative ones. This means that the policies and procedures and generally agreed working practices are underpinned by implicit value statements as to how resources are to be distributed. This illuminates the conflict between managers and practitioners, but does not necessarily imply that discretion is always a positive characteristic (depending on your evaluation of direct payments), as Ellis's research shows. It does, however, point to a degree of freedom that social workers working from an anti-oppressive stance can use positively where they can use their professional discretion to counter the baleful effects of markets and managerialism within social work. Just institutions matter, and therefore social workers wishing to counter the poverty of service users have to assess their organisations from the point of view of their contribution to achieving social justice, and in turn practice to combat this where their organisations are found wanting.

Recommended reading
Harris, J. and White, V. (eds) (2009) *Modernising social work: Critical considerations*, Bristol: Policy Press.

Rothstein, B. (1998) *Just institutions matter: The moral and political logic of the universal welfare state*, Cambridge: Cambridge University Press.

7

Poverty: social division and service users

Although it is not the intention in this chapter to explore individual social divisions such as class, gender and 'race', and to chart their relationship with poverty, this chapter begins by exploring a more complex relationship between the nature of social divisions in society and how they intersect with different service user groups. It then addresses a range of issues not always discussed in relation to poverty or included in social work texts. It does not make the links between poverty and the traditional concerns of poverty studies, for example, higher levels of morbidity and mortality, poor educational attainment and so on. Neither does it link issues such as disability, mental health and learning disability or old age with poverty. However, it covers a range of issues that are seen as controversial within social work, that is, child abuse and poverty, and issues that have been ignored in the social work literature such as lack of food, poor nutrition, obesity and problematic drug use.

Social division and service user status

In a complex global capitalist system people carry different and diverse identities. The intricate social relationships that people now make bring with them different identities that complicate their experience of poverty. Social workers interacting with different service users may encounter this complexity for example between different generations. Second generation Asian migrants who have grown up in the UK may feel less connected to their parents sense of identity which may relate more to their country of origin so that the children of such parents may relate more to the UK and a dual identity as say British Muslim. In order for social workers to frame an appropriate response to poverty, these diverse identities need to be accounted for. Dean (2010) argues that human beings have a fundamental need to be recognised by other human beings in order to have their needs met. As previously discussed, some people from particular groups such as working-class people, people with disabilities, children and so on can be recognised by their 'otherness' (see Chapter 4). Consequently, where these identities may be overlaid by other social categories such as ethnicity and gender, for example, then their particular needs may go unrecognised. As a consequence the policies and procedures of social work and social care organisations may ignore more complex needs and therefore people run the risk of not receiving services attuned to their specific needs.

Social workers interact with service users who belong to broader social divisions such as those of 'race' and class, and how they combine will influence a person's experience of poverty. This result of inter-sectionality, where social divisions coalesce, may then be further influenced by a person's status as a service user, for example, in relation to learning disability. The Department of Health (2009) showed that people with learning disabilities from BME groups and their families often face multiple forms of discrimination, experiencing services that are not sensitive to their needs. A number of reasons are given for this. One is the lack of awareness by professionals on the ground about different cultural needs, a poor understanding of specific disabilities and language barriers. These deficits in services are evidenced in policy and services that are not geared to the needs of different 'races' and cultures that create problems for BME people, particularly in relation to everyday living.

This means that an understanding of both the social location of a service user and the ways in which a service user is categorised into a particular service user group will have consequences for their experience of and access to social work and social care services. In terms of their poverty status and depending on how a service user is categorised may therefore help to ameliorate a service user's social and economic position as opposed to those categorised into a different service user group, which may not do so. An example of this would be to compare an older person who is being rehabilitated to their own home after a lengthy stay in hospital and a person who has been subject to statutory mental health intervention and is now being rehabilitated into the community. A person who has been subject to an order under the Mental Health Act 1983 has a statutory right for help to be rehabilitated back into the community. Health authorities and local social services have a duty to provide rehabilitation for people who have been detained under Sections 3, 37, 47 or 48, but who have left hospital. Under Section 117, a person who has been in hospital under one of the sections mentioned earlier should pay no charge for the services they receive. For an older person coming out of hospital, no such duty exists on behalf of health authorities and social services.

The distribution of poverty between different groups in society is not an even one. Different groups in society therefore experience poverty sometimes in unique ways depending on their relative social positioning in society. For example, rates of poverty reflect a racial divide in the UK so that BME groups are much more likely to be living in poverty. Nearly three quarters of seven-year-old Pakistani and Bangladeshi children and just over half of those black children of the same age are living in poverty; about one in four white seven-year-olds are classed as living in poverty (Institute of Education, 2010). Poverty is also gendered. The Women's Budget Group (2008) reported that about one in every five women in the UK live in poverty, although, as they observe, this is likely to be an underestimate, as poverty is measured in terms of households rather than at the individual level. Therefore these figures do not identify an individual share of income within a household. In addition, where women who care for children often go without necessities such as food and clothing in order to maintain their children, these figures may seriously underestimate the extent of women's poverty.

We can also view poverty through the lens of particular service user groups, for example, children with a learning disability. Emerson and Hatton (2007) found that 47 per cent of children with a learning disability were living in poverty as compared to 30 per cent of all children in the UK. In 30 per cent of their households neither parent was employed compared to 14 per cent of households with children without learning disabilities. Where a child experienced both a learning disability and a mental health problem, 53 per cent of these children lived in poverty. In relation to adults with a learning disability it is highly likely that most adults will be dependent on social security benefits for their entire lives. The Department of Health (2009) identified that one in ten of those known to social services has any form of paid employment, the majority working below 16 hours a week, often amounting to just a few hours. Having briefly outlined the complexity in considering the way a person's social location and their status as a service user interacts, we now consider the links between certain aspects of service users' experience and poverty.

Poverty, child neglect and abuse

Making links between poverty and child neglect and abuse can be highly controversial. Social workers would rightly question any attempt to link these together in any singular way. Yet it is also clear from research and listening to the narratives of service users living in poverty that parents face high levels of stress in coping with poverty and parenting their children. Research also shows that the abuse of children occurs across all social classes (NSPCC, 2008; Bebbington et al, 2011), and that just because a parent may live in poverty, this does not mean that abuse will necessarily follow. However, available research shows an association between poverty and neglect. It is not that poverty causes the neglect of children, but that it is associated with it where other factors may also be present. It is possible that working-class parents, for example, who are more likely to experience poverty, are prone to come to the attention of the police and social work services and receive intervention more than middle-class parents. Research conducted in Australia around issues of therapists' work with sexually violent children showed how class was a defining characteristic in determining what kind of response was made to the child and their abusive parents. Not surprisingly more middle-class families seemed capable of avoiding the attentions of the statutory services and were able to divert treatment into the private sector. However, the workers interviewed, while acknowledging the classlessness of abuse, also reported that the majority of the cases were from families living in poverty. This discourse of classlessness has a positive focus in that it prevents class being used as a defining factor, although it does have a negative, as this discourse supports abuse via intergenerational transmission, that is, the cultural poverty thesis, therefore ignoring social structural causes. Paradoxically, by promoting a culture of poverty, this explanation justifies increased intervention by the statutory authorities for particular working-class families. This discourse may then lead practitioners to become blind to possible structural explanations for poverty and abuse, particularly given the individualistic nature of the intervention promoted within statutory authorities, which is as true of the UK as it is of Australia (Allan, 2006).

In assessing the effect of poverty on child abuse and neglect it is important to separate out the different forms of abuse. It has long been established that there is no correlation or causal link to suggest that poverty is related to child sexual abuse; what is under consideration here is the link between physical abuse and maltreatment or neglect. A recent study from the US explored the link between families on low income and child physical abuse. As Cancian et al (2010) observe, the causal effect of income on maltreatment risk is unknown. Many factors may play a part, for example, poor parental mental health is known to increase the probability of poverty and child maltreatment, so identifying the causal role of income is challenging. However, after comparing families on the Wisconsin Temporary Assistance for Needy Families program who received maximum child support compared to those receiving only partial support, they concluded that those with only partial income support were more likely to be involved in the maltreatment of their children. This is significant if this finding is transferred to the UK in that relatively small increases in income can have an important effect in reducing child maltreatment. As Cancian et al concluded:

> The fact that modest increases in income within an economically disadvantaged population reduced the risk of a screened-in report of child maltreatment suggests that child maltreatment prevention programs should pay explicit attention to the poverty experiences and economic hardships of the families that they serve. (Cancian et al, 2010, p 14)

A study conducted in the UK supports these findings – Sidebotham et al (2002) identified the importance of social deprivation as an important factor determining child maltreatment. There were a number of aspects to this including financial insecurity, housing situation, employment and the richness of social networks; all have a substantial impact on child maltreatment.

This is noteworthy in the light of the Coalition government's contention that their policy towards the relief of poverty will be less focused on income and more about behaviour that impairs social mobility (DWP, 2012a). In practice terms and in order to alleviate the stress of poverty and the risk of child maltreatment, social workers therefore need to focus on increasing a family's income, either through emergency payments in relation to Section 17 of the Children Act 1989 and/or ensuring that a family maximises their income through ensuring maximum entitlement to social security benefit or Universal Credit from work. For those service users with families who may as a result of sanctions being applied to their benefits lose income, the impact on children may have even more serious consequences. It is important for social workers to encourage such service users to apply for hardship grants that are supposed to be available for those affected by benefit sanctions so that any possible consequences can be ameliorated.

Caution does need to be exercised in relation to these studies, however, and the National Society for the Prevention of Cruelty to Children (NSPCC, 2008), in their review of the literature on incidence research in the UK, noted that a number of research problems remain. In particular, a degree of reporting bias may be present in that only those families already known to agencies and experiencing social problems are generally studied. In addition, there are variations in the rates of child protection registrations that do not reflect differences in the nature of the populations or the levels of harm experienced by children.

Food and nutrition

Food policy, as Dowler and O'Connor (2012) argue, is dominated by an individual choice model. The state plays a limited role in regulating the supply of food and maintaining minimum standards of quality within the retail sector. Little recognition is given to the relationship of food quantity and quality to public health or to the right of citizens to access appropriate levels of nutrition.

Social work's concern with poverty should therefore recognise the importance for maintaining health in the ability to buy and access nutritious food for service users and to meet wider social norms of food behaviour. As discussed previously, levels of social security benefit reflect a minimalist account of nutritional need that ignores the practical demands placed on household expenditure (see Chapter 2). Therefore service users living in poverty are almost certain to experience food poverty and food insecurity. Food insecurity involves having insufficient access to an acceptable quality of food combined with an uncertainty that this food can be accessed.

An area often overlooked by social workers is the way in which a lack of adequate food and nutrition is associated with a range of negative outcomes for children. There are two issues that seem relevant: first, a general lack of adequate food that is available that people living in poverty can access; and second, the kind of food those families can afford to eat which can be associated with poor health, such as obesity. It is also important to recognise that obesity is a form of malnutrition. Although it may seem obscene to identify obesity in this way when compared to the experiences of malnourishment and starvation extant in other parts of world, Juby and Meyer (2012) argue that obese children may not look hungry but they do lack the nutrition in their food to maintain optimal health. It seems a cruel irony that malnutrition as obesity hits the poorest in the rich developed world while malnutrition as starvation hits the poorest in the so-called underdeveloped world.

Low-income families' expenditure on food shows that the lowest decile by income spent the highest proportion of their income (23 per cent) on food. Relative prices of fruit and vegetables rose by up to 160 per cent, while soft drinks increased by 26 per cent, less than the rate of inflation, from 1984 to 2002

(Foresight Programme, 2007). Access to cheaper food is also a problem for many poor families who may find it difficult to shop through lacking a car or accessible transport to access out-of-town supermarkets. The Food Standards Agency (2007) found in their survey that 80 per cent of people had access to a major supermarket, with 50 per cent having access to a car for shopping. Where access does appear easier for service users living in poorer neighbourhoods is the preponderance of fast food outlets. As White (2007) observes, McDonald's fast food 'restaurants' were more likely to be found in deprived areas in England and Scotland; this is also the case for other countries such as Australia and the US.

Poorer families who are forced to shop locally find food prices relatively higher than at supermarkets. For poor families, when other demands are made on the family budget, food is often the first casualty as it is the most flexible item to cut back on compared to items such as rent or heating (Dowler, 2003).

> 'You cannot avoid bills. You can't eat when you know you haven't paid your bills.' (quoted in Mitchell et al, 2008, p 19)

Bradshaw et al (2008) found that a couple with two young children on Income Support spent, on average, according to the government Household Expenditure Survey, £67.58 each week, £30 per week less than what 'ordinary' people say is needed to provide a healthy diet. The disparity in levels of income and expenditure on food has not narrowed since then (see Davis et al, 2012).

Given the difficulties faced by individuals and families on a low income in accessing food, the issue of 'food insecurity' is therefore a key concern for such people. Nelson et al (2007) found that 71 per cent of the low-income population they studied reported living in food-secure households. A total of 29 per cent had limited access due to factors such as lack of money, lack of adequate storage facilities or transport at some stage during the year. Thirty-nine per cent of the low-income population reported that, in the last year, they had been worried that their food would run out before they had money to buy more, while 36 per cent indicated that they could not afford to eat balanced meals. The issue of a balanced diet has been commented on by White (2007), who identified research that showed that as families experienced increasing income restraints, the proportion of energy derived from fruit, vegetables and meats declined, and the proportion of cereals, sweets and added fats increased. Mitchell et al's study (2008) of newly migrant workers summarised these issues well: newly migrant workers are often paid at the minimum wage or less with relatively few earning income above this level. Respondents had sufficient knowledge to understand what they should eat, and lack of money to eat within social situations such as eating out added to their social exclusion. But ultimately, of those on the minimum wage or below, for the majority of the respondents:

Under ten percent of the two lowest waged groups feel they can afford to purchase a well-balanced diet or that they can afford to eat five portions of fruit and vegetables a day. (Mitchell et al, 2008, p 3)

The problems of accessing food is not just confined to individuals and families in the community; it is also worth noting the experience of those who may reside in institutions that are either short stay (for example, hospital care) or long term (for example, residential care). The CQC (2011b, p 7) found in their inspection of hospitals that:

Outcome 5: Meeting nutritional needs

Of the 100 checks we made against Outcome 5:
• 51 hospitals were fully compliant.
• 32 were compliant but needed to make improvements.
• 15 were not compliant and had to take action to become compliant.
• Two were a cause of major concern and had to take urgent action.

Where we did find problems, key themes were that:

• Patients were not given the help they needed to eat, meaning they struggled to eat or were physically unable to eat meals.
• Patients were interrupted during meals and had to leave their food unfinished.
• The needs of patients were not always assessed properly, which meant they didn't always get the care they needed – for example, specialist diets.
• Records of food and drink were not kept accurately, so progress was not monitored.
• Many patients were not able to clean their hands before meals.

Standards for food and nutrition cannot therefore always be taken for granted, and require awareness on the part of social workers as to the implications of such food insecurities. Given the difficulties of accessing the right quality of food and the experience of not being able to access food per se, service users in the community are increasingly having recourse to charitable sources such as foodbanks (see below).

Foodbanks: a social work dilemma?

The origins of foodbanks can be traced back to the US where they were developed in the late 1960s to channel surplus food from the food industry to the poor. They took a number of forms, but in terms of this discussion, foodbanks can be defined as charitable organisations that develop places where food is stored to be either distributed by volunteers or made available for collection by service users.

There is a dearth of research in the UK at present on the way that foodbanks operate and the implications for service users who have recourse to them (Lambie, 2011). Yet Riches (2002), writing in the context of Canada, has observed that the emergence and the institutionalisation of charitable operations in food relief is a significant marker for the prevalence of food poverty, signifying the failure of capitalist states' welfare systems to provide sufficient income to purchase adequate levels of food and suggesting that food poverty and rising levels of income inequality go hand in hand. The question for social work and the wider society is to decide how to respond to the emergence of foodbanks and other forms of food charity. The development of foodbanks is beginning to increase in England. Lambie (2011) charts the rise to prominence of The Trussell Trust Foodbank Network: the number of foodbanks developed by the Trust has risen from 20 in 2009 to 148 at the time of publication of the report, with the number of visits to foodbanks having doubled, to over 60,000.

Riches (2002) identifies a number of issues to consider when evaluating the effectiveness of foodbanks in mitigating the effects of food poverty.

Institutionalisation

In Canada the foodbank organisation, the Canadian Association of Food Banks, formed a powerful organisational base that was able to become the sole distributor of food from the large food companies such as Heinz and Quaker Oats. It was also evident that the use of foodbanks had become institutionalised as individuals and families began to seek food on a regular basis. Alongside this, foodbanks became part of the income security programmes nationally across Canada. Likewise, social workers began, as a matter of course, to refer service users to these programmes once they had become established as part of the network of support for poor individuals and families. As Riches (2002, p 7) presciently observes, foodbanks:

> ... have become key institutions in the newly resurrected residual welfare state with Governments relying on them as charitable partners providing feeding programmes of last resort.

Effectiveness

Foodbanks, despite their presence within the social safety net, should be about emergency relief, if they have to operate at all. As emergency relief their role is not to prevent food poverty but to ameliorate it. Surely it is the role of governments to ensure in resource-rich countries such as the UK that their citizens do not go hungry?

Riches' review of the literature suggest that foodbanks are ineffective in the amelioration of food poverty in that the food supplied is often inadequate to prevent families and individuals from going hungry. A recent survey of food service users accessing foodbanks in British Columbia, Canada, found they provided an insufficient diet and:

> ... the food bank clients in our sample ate less than half of the recommended servings of produce daily for individuals 18 years of age and older (7-10 servings daily). In fact, only 8.1% (38/471) of participants consumed 7 or more servings of produce daily. (Holben, 2013, p 456)

So while service users are appreciative of the work of some foodbanks, they did identify that for some organisations the food distributed was not sufficient, lacked variety and was not necessarily the most nutritious. In addition, much research showed that service users felt shame and stigma at having to use foodbanks, and because of the inadequacies of the social security system, had come to use them as part of their regular survival strategies (Riches, 2011).

These considerations have been recognised in the context of the UK. Lambie (2011) notes that there is an important consideration of social justice. Is it acceptable to distribute food that was considered unfit to be sold on a regular basis? She also observed that guidance to organisations in terms of receiving food warned against some suppliers of surplus food who may seek to dump poor quality food onto organisations. Issues of dignity and respect are also important here, and foodbanks, as she argues, should consider the extent to which distributing such food is acceptable in maintaining the dignity of service users. Research conducted in Canada on this issue (Rainville and Brink, 2001), found just one in four hungry Canadians used foodbanks. The research clearly showed that many people would rather go hungry than accept such charity. Recent research from the US (Colby et al, 2010) shows that respondents reported that the barriers to accessing food from foodbanks included embarrassment, lack of transport and an insufficient amount of food provided. Loopstra-Masters and Tarusak's current research (2012, p 497) from Canada reinforces the issue:

> Interviews with 371 low-income Toronto families revealed that 75 percent had experienced some food insecurity, but only 23 percent had used a food bank; for most food bank users, food insecurity was a severe and chronic problem.

For those in need but not using the foodbank, respondents failed to use them because they felt they were not the kind of people to use such a resource, described as reasons of identity (12 per cent), while 11 per cent felt degraded by using such a facility. The majority preferred to get by without recourse to foodbanks (38 per cent), while 22 per cent felt the food was of poor quality, as one respondent describes:

> 'Half the food at the food bank is stuff I don't want. I feel bad being picky, but I would borrow money instead [of going to a food bank]. My children wouldn't eat the food, and the vegetables are not fit to feed an animal. The meats are disgusting and there is too much junk food.' (quoted in Loopstra-Masters and Tarusak, 2012, p 505)

The benefits system in the UK has by default or design encouraged the use of foodbanks. Delayed benefits payments and the increasing use of benefits sanctions is one of the main reasons for accessing this resource. The Trussell Trust (2012), one of the key organisations in the UK coordinating foodbanks, reported that 29 per cent of clients stated that benefits delay was the reason they visited the foodbank. It should be pointed out that The Trussell Trust is a religious-based organisation, which may be a further barrier for some service users, as typically service users are invited to pray with the volunteers when they visit. The concerns raised by Riches in relation to the Canadian experience shows some similarities in the UK.

As McCarthy (2012) observes, The Trussell Trust now appear to be in a formal working relationship with the DWP as job centres formally refer clients to foodbanks when benefits are delayed and they are refused a crisis loan. This relationship is also repeated with children and families departments and other local authority organisations that have contact with such service users.

This relationship raises the question of the role of such state institutions seemingly declining to take responsibility for those in need, and leaving the charitable sector trying to provide some minimal emergency relief.

The acceptability of foodbanks as part of the framework for maintaining a safety net for the poorest members of society is clearly contested. However, as Dowler and O'Connor's (2012) review of food insecurity has pointed out, people on welfare benefits are two to three times more vulnerable to food insecurity than those who are not on social security benefits. In New Zealand, for example, when welfare benefits were cut, the use of foodbanks increased substantially (Stevenson, 2013).

Riches (2002, p 14) is in no doubt that:

> In conclusion, it is clear that the evidence of two decades of food banking in Canada confirms it as an inadequate response to food poverty while allowing Governments to look the other way and neglect hunger and nutritional health.

Exercise

How should social workers respond when service users present as requiring support because they have run out of food?

Commentary

There is no easy answer to this as social workers, on the one hand, will not want to see service users they work with go without food. However, given the analysis previously discussed, it is clear that foodbanks are not the solution. Although social workers need to think about the short-term alleviation of hunger and what this might entail, the longer-term view would be to address the problem of food security. It is interesting to note that problems of fuel poverty have been recognised by successive governments, although there has been an inconsistent recognition on behalf of the energy firms that people cannot be simply cut off unless a clear process has been gone through. Yet it seems that an absence of food has no accepted procedure that would divert people from going hungry.

Assuming that all recourse to Jobcentre Plus and Income Support has been exhausted, service users may well be advised to take this route before alternatives are sought. It is important to ensure that a service user's benefit income is maximised and to ensure that any administrative mistakes have been addressed. This may require the social worker or welfare rights officer advocating on a service user's behalf in relation to the newly localised Social Fund where a crisis loan could be made available. One option for social workers is to exercise their legal duties. Section 17 of the Children Act 1989 defines the duties of a local authority in safeguarding and promoting the general welfare of a child in need and her/his family within their area, and financial assistance can be given to families under this section. Importantly this must be a grant and not a loan, and it is not counted as income by the DWP and does not therefore reduce any weekly benefit. This seems a better course of action in that it enables a service user to spend money on food that is appropriate for them – many people with different dietary needs due to cultural or religious factors are highly unlikely to access appropriate food for their needs from a foodbank unless it has been set up by members of their community.

Social workers can do much at a local level to help service users to access particular programmes and services that may help in providing information and support so that they can be informed and supported in accessing healthier diets. But, as this chapter has argued, without sufficient income as a starting point, service users are always at risk of food poverty. In the longer term social workers need to involve themselves in local and national campaigns to provide adequate social security benefits or support the nationwide take-up, for example, of the Living Wage campaign, examples of which can be seen in London where former Mayor Livingstone and now Mayor Johnson are supporting this through their policies on employment. From looking at the problem of insufficient access to food, this chapter now explores the problem of accessing the wrong type of food.

Obesity

Obesity can be defined as 'an excess of body fat frequently resulting in a significant impairment of health and longevity' (House of Commons Health Committee, 2004). Over the last 20 years the prevalence of obesity across the developed world has doubled in Australia and New Zealand, while in the UK and US it has increased by 50 per cent (NHS Information Centre, 2012).

Being obese or overweight is associated with chronic health problems such as:

- cardiovascular disease
- diabetes
- certain types of cancers
- gallbladder disease. (Wanless, 2004)

As weight increases, so a person's life expectancy decreases, leading to premature death (estimates suggest 30,000 per annum). While obesity is typically age-related – as people get older they put on weight – obesity in children has tripled since 1993. By 2025 it is estimated that 24 per cent of boys and 32 per cent of girls will be overweight. As of now the predicted obesity prevalence for adults shows a difference in relation to class, with 34 per cent of those in the manual class identified as obese compared to 29 per cent in the non-manual classes (NHS Information Centre, 2012). The most comprehensive evidence for a link between poverty and obesity comes from the US Department of Health and Human Services (2012), which shows that low-income children and adults are more likely to be obese than those from higher incomes. Although it is difficult to show the exact causal links, there is a wealth of evidence from across the globe that suggests that this relationship is significant. On a country-wide basis the work of Wilkinson and Pickett (2010) shows that countries across the globe with higher levels of income inequality show an associated higher level of obesity in their populations. The effect of social inequality on obesity is significantly underestimated, according to Samani-Radia and McCarthy (2011). They argue that the method of measuring obesity is floored as the accepted method of calculating a person's Body Mass Index (BMI) does not account totally for fat present in the person; for example, a body builder (using BMI as a measure) would be considered obese. A more appropriate method would be to calculate the percentage of body fat present. Although childhood obesity rates are reported to be levelling off, Samani-Radia and McCarthy's research shows that children from lower-income homes are nearly twice as likely to be overweight or obese as those from higher-income homes. They found that by measuring the percentage of body fat instead of BMI, the income difference between the children became greater. This is a more accurate measure as, even though the lower-income children were shorter for their age and had higher body fat levels, a large number of them had been deemed as 'normal weight' by their BMI.

Obesity and anti-oppressive practice

Social workers need to be aware of the way in which children and adults may be increasingly discriminated against because of their size and weight. Government policy also mirrors this in the way that it focuses on a person's lifestyle, assuming that for many people obesity is a choice rather than contextualising the problem and focusing on the structures in society that reinforce ill health and poverty. Given that obesity is a global phenomenon, to focus purely on an individual's responsibility for the lifestyle they lead overlooks these wider social relations. As the Royal College of Physicians' briefing statement (2005, p 2) identifies:

- People on low incomes eat more processed foods that are much higher in saturated fats and salt.
- They also eat less variety of foods. This is related to economies of scale and fear of potential waste.
- People living on state benefits eat less fruit and vegetables, less fish and less high-fibre breakfast cereals.
- People in the UK living in households without an earner consume more total calories, and considerably more fat, salt and non-milk extrinsic sugars than those living in households with one or more earners.

Such extrinsic factors are rarely addressed in the discourse from government and the media when talking about obesity. The food and fast food industry have a clear commercial interest in promoting the idea of individual choice and consumption of fast food (Dowler, 2003). The ideology of individual responsibility for food consumption contains strong moral condemnation of the poor, as Townend (2010) argues is reflected in the issue of obesity, where social 'obesogenic' factors, such as media advertising of fast food, contribute to the eating choices made by individuals.

Social workers need to be wary of blaming adults or the parents of children when considering obesity. Concern has been raised about some interventions within this context where discussions have revolved around whether obesity in relation to children is a child protection issue. A British Medical Journal (BMJ, 2010) editorial discussed the proposal of a framework to be used when obesity should be considered a child protection issue. The doctors concerned argued that obesity of itself is not a child protection issue but they argued that there is growing evidence linking adolescent and adult obesity with childhood sexual abuse, violence and neglect. As a result, they recommended that social workers should intervene when parents fail to engage with treatment for their child's obesity when there is a risk of illness, and should be aware that for children who are very obese, this could be symptomatic of other forms of abuse.

Clearly social workers should be vigilant when children's health is in danger, but they also need to be aware of the ways in which the obesogenic culture in the society in which we live encourages obesity by limiting access by the poor to more nutritious foods. Thus, in distinction to the argument raised within the BMJ, social workers' first concern should be, all other things being equal, to see obesity as a problem of child and family support rather than as a protection issue, and to make strenuous efforts to encourage families to be able to access better quality food. This is both to increase the incomes of households to enable the purchase of healthier food and to enable parents to be able to see the value of such an approach. At current benefit levels (mentioned earlier) it is virtually impossible to purchase a healthy diet as it requires extra income and a constant search to access healthy food which goes beyond the capacity of most individuals living in poverty.

The annual Food Survey makes uncomfortable reading for those wishing to deal with the problem of obesity. Expenditure on food was £27.99 per person in 2011, an increase of 1.5 per cent, but this bought 4.2 per cent less food. In order to manage the food budget, households saved 6.8 per cent by trading down to cheaper and in many cases less healthy foods that were higher in salt and fat content. The poorest households spent a greater proportion of their income on food compared to all households, and among the poorest households the consumption of every major nutrient has fallen (DEFRA, 2012).

Obesity is not therefore a lifestyle choice but is intimately linked to inequality and the obesogenic culture that reflects it. Different approaches therefore need to be developed that do not blame individuals but rather support individuals and families to access more healthy food. This may require a broader community approach which develops, for example, community food cooperatives or community gardens whereby service users can use their collective buying power, and time to access healthier food; these have been successful in the US and Canada (Loopstra-Masters and Tarasuk, 2012; Holben, 2013).

Substance misuse and poverty

In describing substance misuse this section focuses on illegal drug use. This is not to minimise the role that alcohol and cigarettes play in the wider field of drug use and the damage they cause, but the focus is on an area that has not received significant attention within social work services (Galvani and Hughes, 2010).

Drug addiction is rare. Although many people use illegal drugs, only a minority become so dependent as to be addicted. It is estimated that there are three million people in England using drugs, of which some 300,000 use more problematic drugs, such as heroin and crack cocaine, over half of these people are in treatment. As of 2012, the use of some problematic drugs, such as heroin, is on the decline. The numbers of people who began to use heroin and crack cocaine in the 1980s and early 1990s is now shrinking, and younger people are tending not to use these drugs but other kinds of illegal stimulants (National Treatment Agency for Substance Misuse, 2012).

Social workers work on a regular basis with service users who are linked to problematic substance use; research suggests the high prevalence of drug misuse among service users of social work services. Service users who misuse drugs can be found across the lifespan, although long-term drug users are increasingly likely to be found in adults and older people's services; for example, the over-40s represent the largest group of heroin users. Social work responses in this area are limited, and this is recognised in *Every Child Matters: Change for children* (2004) that identifies 'substance misuse' among young people as one area that requires improvements in the development of services. The absence of policy and recognition in practice is also mirrored in social work education and training where substance misuse is often a missing aspect on social work education programmes (Galvani and Hughes, 2010). By comparison, attention to drug misuse has been a significant concern for the criminal justice system, including the Probation Service (see Buchanan, 2010).

The link between poverty and problematic drug use is a complex issue, but there are causal pathways that highlight the relevance of investigating this relationship. Not all people living in poverty will misuse drugs, but those living on the margins of society, such as homeless people and care leavers, are more susceptible. Likewise, problematic drug misuse can be found across the social spectrum. However, the problem for many people living in deprived neighbourhoods is that their problematic drug use is more visible, as they are subject to more state surveillance and control either by the police, social workers or drug workers. Coping with the consequences of using such drugs is harder if you lack income resulting in poor access to specialist health services and counselling which you may have to pay for to avoid delay in treatment. Thus, as Seddon (2006) has argued, the link between drug misuse poverty and social exclusion reflects choices made by individuals, but within a set of constrained social circumstances. Or, as Shaw et al (2007, pp 11-12) argue:

> Deprivation does not directly cause addiction, instead it increases the propensity to misuse – it weakens what are sometimes called the protective factors and it strengthens the risk factors. So even though the causes of deprivation are social, they are experienced individually.

The impact of poverty on under-resourced communities, a lack of income and widening inequality are all factors that need to be given a more central role in the discussion. In Scotland, Shaw et al (2007), for example, showed that the overall unemployment rate of new contacts seeking help from drug services has averaged out at an annual rate of 85 per cent – a stark contrast to the national unemployment rate at the time of the study, which was 5.2 per cent. It has been estimated that 80-90 per cent of all Scottish prisoners taken into custody have been misusing drugs and/or alcohol, and that significantly high rates of prisoners come from the most deprived council ward areas. Problematic drug use is not only a consequence of such social factors as social exclusion and poverty, but it is also a factor in developing such poor social outcomes as living in long-term poverty in the future. Larm et al's (2008) research into adolescents examined the prevalence of death, physical illnesses related to substance misuse, mental illness, substance misuse, criminality and poverty in adulthood among two cohorts of individuals who, as adolescents, had consulted for substance misuse problems. They found:

- In the older cohort followed to age 50, only one-in-five escaped all six adverse outcomes, while over half of subjects experienced at least two or more.
- Sex and the severity of adolescent substance misuse and delinquency were predictors of adverse outcomes.

- More women than men experienced physical illness and poverty in the older cohort while more men than women were convicted of criminal offences in both cohorts and presented continued substance misuse in the younger cohort.
- Men in the younger as compared to the older cohort had higher rates of substance misuse and criminal convictions.

They concluded that adolescents who sought help for substance misuse problems are at an elevated risk for multiple adverse outcomes later in life. Outcomes differ for women and men and by the severity of adolescent misuse and delinquency.

Governmental response to drug misuse has, in the view of some commentators, recognised that this is not solely a medical or criminal issue. The previous Labour government, as Buchanan (2010) has argued, did recognise the need to address the structural and personal problems associated with drug misuse, yet the outcome of Labour's time in government was to see the deepening and widening of inequality with a failure to meet its self-imposed targets on reducing poverty.

The impact of problematic drug use

The use of illicit drugs by one member of a family has a destructive impact on other members. The parents of children who engage in problematic drug use evidence signs of deteriorating physical and mental ill health. Other siblings are also affected as their brother or sister may introduce them to taking drugs. Family relationships become focused on the person using drugs and therefore relationships become skewed as the drug user becomes the focus of the entire family (Barnard, 2005).

Drug use has a wider communal impact as drugs are bought and sold within the communities where demand is highest. At the level of the community the conditions for a drug market to develop are two-fold. One condition is associated with highly fragmented neighbourhoods where the local infrastructure, in terms of local resources, is depleted; in many ways this represents the stereotype of a community where drugs are bought and sold. However, highly cohesive yet deprived neighbourhoods also provide the opportunity to develop a drug market. As May et al (2005) argue, by the very nature of their networks, closely-knit communities in deprived areas may have some of the preconditions needed for markets to develop. Drug markets provide opportunities for some people to earn money in areas that are blighted by high levels of unemployment. In many ways the social relations of production within these markets parallel those within more legitimate labour markets, with a small group of highly paid professional dealers earning in the region of £7,500 a week, employing a network of small-time dealers on the streets to distribute the product, earning £450 per week. May et al (2005) interviewed a number of people who were involved in selling in the four drug markets they investigated, and found that the majority (75 per cent) were men in their early thirties, a third of whom had lived in the area where they dealt drugs. Their social backgrounds were telling in relation to social work:

> Many had experienced unsettled early lives: over half had lived with a foster family, in a children's home or in secure accommodation. Interviewees had typically used alcohol and illicit drugs from an early age. Many had had a disrupted education, over half being excluded from school or leaving with no educational qualifications. Nearly all had been in contact with the criminal justice system, and over two-thirds had served a prison sentence. (May et al, 2005, p 4)

Because many users live in the same neighbourhoods as the drug markets, those users wishing to move into employment face considerable barriers, both in terms of finding employment in areas of high deprivation and also where opportunities to access drugs were readily available. Klee et al (2002) found similar social histories to May et al (2005), with high proportions of respondents having been in care, or raised by single parents, and moving house had often led to school disruption with significant experiences of bullying at school and high levels of truancy. Although the majority of respondents wanted a job, many feared a drop in income as they were in receipt of Sickness or Invalidity Benefit and the kinds of employment open to them would not compensate them in order to come off benefits. Many also lost hope in realising that if they had a criminal record, as most did, that this would prevent a real chance of permanent work.

The nature of the relationship between drug misuse and poverty can be seen as a symbiotic relationship where one feeds off the other. For Buchanan (2004), drug misuse can be seen as a form of escape from an oppressive social environment, particularly for those who use drugs in early adulthood. This sense of exclusion is then heightened by the way in which drug misuse is responded to by wider societal reaction, for example, criminalising such behaviour rather than attempting rehabilitation. This in turn reinforces the exclusion of young people who, as a consequence, find it harder to re-join society (Buchanan, 2004). At a macro level Wilkinson and Pickett (2010) have shown how societies with greater income and wealth inequalities experience greater involvement in problematic drug misuse and heightened levels of criminal activity. The widening gap between people in relation to income and wealth may lead to adverse stress related to worsening social conditions of those at lower levels of income. This then develops certain negative responses such as poor health outcomes, lack of choice and an increase in problematic drug use.

Children and families and misuse of drugs

One of the key areas of concern for social workers is the role of parents who are misusing drugs. It has been estimated that there are between 250,000 and 350,000 children of problematic drug users in the UK, and a third of adults in treatment have childcare responsibilities (Cleaver et al, 2011). Issues often involve the capacity of parents to meet the needs of their children, sometimes leading to more serious cases where problematic drug use is related to child neglect and abuse. Yet, as Cleaver et al argue, no systematic research has been carried out to investigate the association between misuse of drugs and child abuse.

In their literature review Cleaver et al highlight a number of findings showing particular associations in this area:

• Parental abuse of drugs or alcohol, or both, is found in more than half of parents who neglect their children.
• Research that explores the association between parental problem drug misuse and child abuse suggests parental drug use is generally associated with neglect and emotional abuse.
• Parents who experience difficulty in organising their own and their children's lives are unable to meet children's needs for safety and basic care; they become emotionally unavailable to them and have difficulties in controlling and disciplining their children.

For parents who may be coming off using drugs through the use of methadone, for example, the effect on social functioning is minimal, and many are able to work in areas of great responsibility and raise their families.

In responding to issues of drug misuse, children and family social workers need to maintain a clear focus on the parenting capacity of parents who misuse drugs. This requires workers assessing the impact of the parents' drug use on their parenting skills in order to providing support if parenting is impaired. It may also require, where social workers feel that children are at risk, that they use their statutory powers but only as a last resort. However, as Harwin et al (2011) show, the current responses by social workers in using care proceedings may be highly damaging to children and their parents. Harwin et al's evaluation of a pilot project in dealing with these issues by using what are called Family Drug and Alcohol Courts (FADCs) shows a more constructive and holistic approach that can be more effective in working with children and their parents. It is important to outline the holistic nature of such a project as it considers both the intervention through the courts alongside wider social intervention.

> FDAC is a specialist problem-solving court operating within the framework of care proceedings, with parents given the option of joining the pilot. Working with the court is a specialist, multi-disciplinary team of practitioners. The team carry out assessments, devise and co-ordinate an individual intervention plan, help parents engage and stay engaged with substance misuse and parenting services, carry out direct work with parents, get feedback on parental progress from services, and provide regular reports on parental progress to the

court and to all others involved in the case. Attached to the team are volunteer parent mentors to provide support to parents.

Cases in FDAC are heard by two dedicated district judges, with two further district judges available to provide back up for sickness and holidays. Cases are dealt with by the same judge throughout. Guardians are appointed to FDAC cases immediately. Legal representatives attend the first two court hearings, but thereafter there are regular, fortnightly, court reviews which legal representatives do not attend, unless there is a particular issue requiring their input. The court reviews are the problem-solving, therapeutic aspect of the court process. They provide opportunities for regular monitoring of parents' progress and for judges to engage and motivate parents, to speak directly to parents and social workers, and to find ways of resolving problems that may have arisen. (Harwin et al, 2011, p 4)

The evaluation compared families using the FDAC with those taken through 'normal' care proceedings; there were encouraging results in respect to the FDAC:

1. FDAC parents were more likely to have stopped misusing substances;
2. more children on the FDAC programme were reunited with their families;
3. the level of costs associated with FDAC were lower;
4. children of FDAC cases spent less time in out-of-home placements.

Parents who used the service were generally very positive about the programme, with all but two parents saying they would recommend the programme to other parents in a similar situation. Buchanan and Corby (2005) explored the problems of working with child protection issues, highlighting the different values that different professionals had regarding drug misuse, and recommended a greater awareness of these differences if effective interagency working was to be achieved. It is clear that the FDAC programme offers an opportunity for professionals to work together in a constructive way with children and parents that accounts for the individual factors of drug misuse within a wider community partnership of professionals who can bring their expertise to bear. In relation to the views of service users, Buchanan and Corby (2005) identified what service users valued in terms of intervention. Most important was the style and approach of professionals in engaging with service users. The following was identified:

• the importance of professional consistency;
• the importance of open and honest communication;
• the need for workers to be comfortable with the issue of drugs;
• the need to be viewed realistically and not harshly or negatively.

Shaw et al's review of the link between poverty and drug misuse in Scotland concludes:

> Although relative poverty by itself is not the cause of Scotland's drug problem, this literature review supports the view that there is a strong association between the extent of drug problems and a range of social and economic inequalities. (Shaw et al, 2007, p 45)

Social workers therefore need an awareness of the wider impact of poverty on drug misuse and the way that this is then reflected in the way individuals decide on and maintain or not their drug dependency within this context. Developing effective responses that deal with the individual presentation of the consequences of drug misuse, for example, in relation to parenting capacity within this broader perspective, holds out a better outcome for service users. The Scottish Executive (2006) has produced a useful guide for social workers wishing to adopt such an approach.

Summary

This chapter began by recognising the complex relationships between people's social location and their status as social work service users. It then explored a number of issues in relation to the status of service users that have been relatively ignored by social work. Issues such as access to food and obesity, for example, are not the product of individual lifestyle choices but are intimately linked with the structure of society within which people make their choices. The choice to use illegal drugs shows a remarkable consistency in that it is those with the least control over resources who often find themselves subject to social work intervention. It is within this context that social workers need to be aware of this complex relationship between personal choices that people make and the context within which they make them.

Recommended reading

Dowler, E. and O'Connor, D. (2012) 'Rights-based approaches to addressing food poverty and food insecurity in Ireland and UK', *Social Science & Medicine*, vol 74, pp 44-51.

May, T., Duffy, M., Few, B. and Hough, M. (2005) *Understanding drug selling in local communities*, York: Joseph Rowntree Trust.

8

Globalisation, social work and poverty

This chapter investigates the impact of globalisation on social work and considers the effects of globalisation on those service users living in poverty. In particular it looks at the position of asylum seekers, those who have been trafficked into the UK and issues affecting those who migrate to work in the UK.

Globalisation

Globalisation is a contested concept. Writers such as Pugh and Gould (2000) argue that to contend that globalisation is a unique stage of development is invalid; they point to an enduring continuity in the way that trade has always been undertaken on an international basis. Hirst et al (2009) argue in a similar vein that globalisation as such is a myth. Others, such as the World Trade Organization (WTO), work towards promoting global free trade and in doing so argue that this contributes to economic prosperity and social welfare among nation states. As Pascal Lamy, Director General of WTO, argues, globalisation can be successfully harnessed to alleviate poverty and to complement the development of social welfare within states (quoted in Bacchetta and Jansen, 2011). Writing from a critical perspective, Ferguson and Woodward (2009) have argued for the baleful effects of globalisation on the ability of nation states to determine their own destinies. For these writers (see also Harvey, 2005), globalisation reflects a neo-liberal project that has as its aim the reduction of government spending on welfare and other social projects, the maximisation of corporate profit and the accumulation of wealth in the hands of a privileged minority. As a consequence, these processes are increasing the levels of poverty and social inequality across the globe.

This book contends that globalisation is a real and potent force which is transforming the way in which nation states operate and which has unparalleled influence over the way in which social policies in these countries are sustained and developed. Globalisation, through the evidence discussed later, does little to enhance the welfare of those affected by it. Social workers in the UK are increasingly confronted with the human consequences of such a process that has and will in the future transform their lives and the lives of the service users with whom they work.

Much of the economic debate in relation to globalisation has focused on the power of multinational companies to wield their global corporate power over nation states. Business interests have always played a significant role in the shaping of social policy, but recent developments within an increasingly globalised world have shown how this power is becoming more ubiquitous. The role of globalisation cannot be overestimated; in regard to decisions that promote social welfare, most welfare decisions are made dependent on whether they contribute to the productive process or not. As Farnsworth and Holden argue:

> In many respects, there has been little need for organised business and firms to seek to influence social policy during recent years since, in most ways and in most areas, social policy has been steered in a pro-business direction by politicians. Structural influences, reinforced by globalisation, have promoted cuts in spending on unproductive services and expansion in productive services. (2006, p 482)

Social policy has been steered in a pro-business direction by politicians of all political persuasions who interpret the needs of business as being almost synonymous with the needs of society. The current Prime Minster, David Cameron, while noting that globalisation has winners and losers, nevertheless calls for more openness and competition in world trade:

> Politicians need to understand the realities of life for the entrepreneur and wealth creator.... In the globalised world, the battle for competitiveness will not be won through impassioned argument about the benefits of an open economy. It will be won through competent implementation of the conditions of an open economy. (Cameron, 2006)

The power of what can be called corporate welfare operates at many levels of the economy and society but represents a significant transfer of resources to this sector and a further reduction in resources for social welfare (Farnsworth, 2012). This process of transfer, from the social to the economic, is increasingly setting the context for the way in which globalisation has an impact on social work.

In the present economic crisis the Coalition government's determination to limit public expenditure means the opportunities for local and global capital to provide privatised welfare will increase. As a result of the government's Spending Review in 2010, local governments face significant cutbacks over the intervening four-year period. The DCLG will experience a 27 per cent cut in its local government budget and a 51 per cent cut in its communities budget between 2010-14 (Lowndes and Pratchett, 2012). Within social work services the opportunities for further privatisation are likely to increase as local authorities look to limit their operations to what may be minimally required in terms of their statutory requirements. However, it may not be limited even to these functions; for example, elements of statutory childcare can also be outsourced. There are currently a number of pilot projects that seek to extend privatisation into children's services (Stanley et al, 2012). The proposals to develop more privatised forms of Probation Services at no extra cost for released prisoners are an example where the Probation Service will supervise more serious offenders while those who have served lesser sentences will be supported by private and voluntary sector providers (Ministry of Justice, 2013).

Globalisation defined

Globalisation can be understood as a process that has a number of dimensions:

- political
- economic
- social and cultural.

Political

The political impact of globalisation has been identified in the way that nation states' autonomy, that is, their ability to control their own foreign and domestic policies, has been compromised by increasing pressure from the wider economic and political forces of globalisation. As a cause and effect of this, wider organisations of global governance have been developed to institute decision making beyond the nation state, for example, the European Community and the United Nations. In so far as these bodies reflect the globalisation of political processes, they also hold within them attempts to manage globalisation, albeit within a limited framework of capitalist social relations. However, globalisation, as Yeates (2001) argues, can also create new spaces for forms of resistance and new ways to organise such as the Anti-Globalisation Movement or in terms of social work, issues in the form of global service user movements and the International Federation of Social Workers.

Economic

The economic impact of globalisation refers to the increasing global nature of economic processes such as the worldwide production and exchange of goods and services. Deregulation of nation states' economies by limiting such regulations as health and safety requirements makes those states, as it is argued by supporters of global free trade, open to inward investment. However, critics of global free trade argue that this is rather mythical in that the economically dominant nations can protect their industries through subsidies and tariff controls (for example, in the case of the US in agriculture and textiles), while requiring the less powerful to open up their economies to free trade. Large corporations have argued for trade restrictions to be placed on developing nations that fail to enforce intellectual property rights, particularly in the area of computer technology. Without access to such items as software packages, their ability to compete may be compromised (Hill and Rapp, 2009).

In terms of economic policy, governments belong to a number of forums that regulate their economic policy, particularly in developing free trade. One of the key organisations in determining economic policy is the General Agreement on Tariffs and Trade (GATT), which is part of the WTO and is now commonly referred to as GATS (General Agreement on Trade in Services). The provisions of GATS covers all service sectors, from banking, energy and telecommunications to predominantly public services such as prisons, water delivery, healthcare and education. The GATS mandate is that services essential to human life and social stability be increasingly exposed to the vagaries of international markets. Commitments governments make under GATS are practically irreversible. These commitments can be explored through what are termed services agreements. These were originally advanced by a small group of major US corporations – American Express and Citicorp were instrumental in promoting the adoption of GATS in 1994. This began the process of opening up nation states' public services for exploitation by major health corporations, particularly from the US – for example, these corporations have been instrumental in the buying up of residential care homes in the South of England, as have major European venture capital investment banks (Scourfield, 2007).

Social and cultural

With the increase in the capability of computer technology to move, process and store information, space and time becomes compressed so that people communicate across time zones and national borders without being physically present with one another. People have the opportunity to access the latest branded goods and consume a wide range of consumer products that are made available online. The spread of global brands can have an impact on local cultures, a process termed McDonaldisation (Dustin, 2007), in which the dominance of powerful global brands can potentially homogenise, for example, people's consumption of food, clothing and music. The spread of information across the globe means that previous cultural influences spread out from those countries with the resources to do so. In social work, for example, this has led to a vigorous debate in relation to determining global standards and the possible impact of Western approaches to social work on other nation states and their cultures (Sewpaul, 2005).

Globalisation and social work

Having briefly introduced the concept of globalisation, the rest of this chapter focuses on how globalisation has resulted in new challenges to social work services from those people seeking asylum and those people who are trafficked across borders to work in service industries and the sex trade, all of whom experience poverty in its starkest from.

Refugees and asylum seekers

In 2011 the four countries from which the bulk of people were seeking asylum in the UK came from Afghanistan, Iran, Sri Lanka and Pakistan, while applications from Syria have also increased significantly (Refugee Council, 2012). All these countries have experienced major conflicts and as a consequence significant violence has been perpetrated on their populations. As a result, people feeling under threat from these conflicts often have to leave very quickly, leaving their family, friends and possessions behind. Crawley (2010) found in her research that the majority of people she interviewed had been in fear of their lives in their home countries, and had only a few days or weeks to get to a place of safety. Many of her respondents did not know which country they would arrive at, and had not necessarily chosen to come to the UK.

A person is considered a refugee when the Home Office accepts their application for asylum. A person is classed as an asylum seeker when a claim has been lodged with the UK Border Agency (UKBA) at the Home Office, and the person is awaiting a decision on their claim. If the asylum application is granted, the refugee is granted limited leave to stay, initially for five years, after which their case is reviewed. This applies to those who have received refugee status since September 2005; before this date refugees were allowed to remain indefinitely. This represents a further toughening of the law in this regard since 2005; indeed, over the past 25 years, successive government policy in the UK towards asylum seekers has resulted in making entry into the UK increasingly difficult, with entitlement to a range of social rights being withdrawn, leading to the widespread destitution of asylum seekers as a result (Spicer, 2008). In particular, access to adequate income and housing has been particularly restricted. Most claims for asylum are initially refused (68 per cent in 2011), but many appeals succeed (26 per cent in 2011) (Home Office, 2012); this reinforces the argument that decisions taken regarding the granting of asylum are particularly restrictive, which must lead to a questioning of the impartiality and the quality of those initial decisions (Gillespie, 2012).

The Immigration and Asylum Act 1999 enforced a system of dispersal with asylum seekers moved to designated areas in the UK aimed, it was argued, at limiting pressure on welfare and housing services in the South East of England. The practice of dispersal results in asylum seekers often moved to areas with high concentrations of unemployment, poor housing and risk of exclusion by some sections of the local population. A study carried out by the Refugee Media Action Group (2006) examined the living conditions of 50 asylum seekers living in and around London. The study identified widespread problems with the quality of the housing they experienced, which included discriminatory attitudes of housing staff, damp, infestation and leaking ceilings, poor heating and cooking facilities.

Spicer's research encapsulates the experience of dispersal well in relation to the racial harassment experienced by one family:

> The mother described their isolation and uncertainty in that neighbourhood: "... I was alone, I didn't know what was going to happen, where I was going to go". The family experienced high levels of "racial harassment" and "bullying" and they were afraid to leave the house: "[... people were] ... targeting Asians and people, who weren't,

you know, white.... In the first couple of months I hardly went out of the house." (Spicer, 2008, p 496)

By definition, to be an asylum seeker means that you will be poor through no fault of your own. The impoverishment of asylum seekers is caused by government policy that has deliberately reduced asylum seekers' income to below basic entitlement for a range of social security benefits. People with no children who are refused asylum lose financial support 21 days after the refusal of their claim. Some asylum seekers receive Section 4 support (Asylum and Immigration Act 1999) if they are destitute and willing but unable to return to their country of origin. Section 4 support is paid in specific circumstances to destitute people refused asylum; included within this is accommodation. Voucher cards (known as the Azure card) to buy basic food and a limited set of essential items are issued only when accommodation is in place. The extent of the financial pressure on asylum seekers can be gauged by the amount paid on the Azure card, which, for a single person in 2012, was £35.36, while the equivalent level for a single person over the age of 25 receiving Income Support was £71.00.

Smart and Fullegar (2008) conducted research with the Inter-Agency Partnership (IAP) and asked their One Stop Services to record the proportion of people using these services who were destitute. Caseworkers defined 'destitute' as those with no access to benefits/Border and Immigration Agency [now UKBA] support/income and who were either homeless (living on the street) or living with friends. The research found that:

- 44 per cent (1,524 of 3,466 cases) of the people using the services of refugee agencies were destitute;
- 27 per cent of the destitute cases were people pursuing a claim for asylum and so were likely to be legally entitled to support but not receiving it because of procedural errors.

Refused asylum seekers made up the majority of destitute cases (58 per cent). In addition, a number of people (6 per cent) were destitute because they wished to claim asylum but had not yet been able to register their claim. The destitution of these people runs counter to the requirements of European Council Directive 2003/9/EC, 'Laying down minimal standards for the reception of asylum seekers', which requires European Union (EU) member states to provide support and accommodation for asylum seekers.

The conditions relating to asylum seekers' access to adequate income and housing are therefore part of a deliberate policy to deter those seeking asylum (Gillespie, 2012). Asylum seekers are generally not allowed to work, so that any attempt to increase their income means that any work they may find will be in the informal illegal economy, usually involving dangerous and unregulated work. As previously discussed, benefit levels are up to half that of Income Support levels and no additional income is available to parents who have older children (16–17 years old) and for children with disabilities (The Children's Society, 2012). For social workers this poses some fundamental problems as the UKBA has a statutory duty under Section 55 of the Borders, Citizenship and Immigration Act 2009 to safeguard and promote children's welfare relating to Section 55 statutory guidance: *Every Child Matters: Change for children* (November 2009). Local authorities have a general duty to support children in need in their area; likewise, children seeking asylum alone are usually looked after under Section 20 of the legislation. Social services can provide accommodation and other help if this is required to safeguard or promote the child's welfare, yet support can be withheld from those deemed ineligible, such as refused asylum seekers. Local authorities tend to only provide support to children deemed destitute; parents will not receive help. In practice parents seeking support are either turned away or may be threatened with having their children taken into care.

Local authorities are required to inform the Home Office when they consider someone to be an 'ineligible person'; many parents and young people fear their removal and so do not access any help from the local authority (Pinter, 2012).

Once an asylum seeker is refused asylum they are given an entitlement to income; this is accessed via the Azure card that replaced the voucher system in 2009. This card is topped up weekly and any money left over, above £5 per week, cannot be carried forward. The card is not popular, least of all because people feel the indignity and shame of being marked out in this way when using the card in supermarkets. The problem is further exacerbated as only some supermarkets accept the card and therefore asylum seekers may face longer than normal journeys in order to shop where the card is accepted. In addition, the card only allows the purchase of essential food items; non-essential items such as toiletries and children's clothing cannot be purchased using this system. Likewise, failed asylum seekers cannot purchase travel tickets to see legal representatives with this card and nor can they buy telephone cards to contact them. As Reynolds (2010) observes:

> The UKBA argues that people supported under Section 4 do not need such items as they should only be in receipt of support for a short period of time. However, our evidence shows that many people are supported under Section 4 for a prolonged period of time and, therefore, it cannot be considered a short-term support mechanism. 38% of our respondents (34) have been in receipt of Section 4 support for over two years. The effect of denying these purchases is the gradual erosion of the dignity and self-esteem of refused asylum seekers.

In essence, asylum seekers find themselves living in destitution. Definitions of destitution vary; for example, the Immigration and Asylum Act 1999 identifies that a person is destitute if they lack adequate accommodation or the means of obtaining it whether or not other essential living needs are met; or the person has adequate accommodation or the means of obtaining it, but cannot meet other essential living needs. Other definitions include lack of access to statutory support or requiring the help of friends, family or charities to make ends meet (Morrell and Wainwright, 2006). Nevertheless, many of the studies included in this section all attest to the fact that asylum seekers experience the most extreme forms of destitution (see Reynolds, 2010; Crawley, 2012; Gillespie, 2012; Pinter, 2012).

Social work and asylum seekers

Social work has been slow to respond to the needs of asylum seekers, particularly those placed within local authorities who, as mentioned earlier, provide limited and patchy support, even to children covered by the provisions of the Children Act 1989. Gillespie's research in Scotland revealed, for example, that of the 811 respondents she studied between 2009-12, only two received any social work support, and this despite the fact that at every stage of the asylum process respondents were experiencing delays in receiving entitlement to benefits, which meant that they were living in various stages of destitution and therefore experiencing extreme poverty and homelessness. As one researcher observes, analysis of the data:

> ... illustrates how the risk of destitution arises throughout the asylum support process. Administrative and procedural problems in this complex system and extremely short timescales for transitions from one stage to another appear to be difficult to meet for the United Kingdom Border Agency and other providers as much as for asylum seekers. (Gillespie, 2012, p 32)

There are social and emotional consequences for asylum seekers existing on an inadequate income and living in poor housing or worse, sleeping in shelters or in friends' houses. By definition, the dispersal system means that support networks become fragmented, and asylum seekers talk of the experience of isolation and loneliness when they are unable to have close contact with friends and family. Some asylum seekers may also be experiencing the effects of trauma brought on by their experiences of seeing loved ones killed in front of them or of being raped or tortured in the countries from which they have fled. The sense of loss and guilt at having escaped from such situations bears heavily on their emotional and mental health. The quotation below illustrates how this emotional strain is experienced:

> 'Feeling good about myself? Maybe I can explain it. Because of my situation, because of what I'm going through – and much has happened to me – and my result at the moment, it makes me just feel useless at the moment, like I am not being appreciated, so I don't feel good at all.'
>
> 'Always I am tense, because I cannot stay here, but I cannot go to my country.' (quoted in Gillespie, 2012, pp 41-2)

The Social Care Institute for Excellence (SCIE) (2010) has produced guidance on how social work and social care should support asylum seekers. The approach is rights-based, in which the responsibility of social work and social care is firmly rooted in countering the denial of such rights as they exist within the current asylum system. This can be evidenced by Schedule 3 of the Nationality, Immigration and Asylum Act 2002 which prevents local authorities from routinely providing support to refused asylum seekers who are in the country unlawfully. However, they do not prevent local authorities providing assistance to refused asylum seekers if to do otherwise would be a breach of an individual's human rights under the Human Rights Act 1998. There are a number of flexible provisions that should be considered for adults where need is assessed and met by developing direct payments or a personal budget.

The Children Act 1989 places a number of duties on local authorities, all of which apply to asylum seekers:

• Section 17 gives local authorities a duty to provide support for children in need.
• Section 20 gives them a duty to provide accommodation for children who require it.
• Section 31 gives local authorities a duty to investigate and take action if it is believed that children are in need of protection.

Child asylum seekers who are 'looked-after children' are entitled to formal planning and independent review of their care. They are also entitled to services under the Children (Leaving Care) Act 2000 and associated regulations, which define their eligibility.

As previously discussed, the Children Act 2004 now includes a duty on local authorities to improve the wellbeing of all children in their area and to make arrangements to safeguard and promote their welfare (Sections 10 and 11). However, Section 9 of the Asylum and Immigration (Treatment of Claimants, etc) Act 2004 allows the withdrawal of support to families whose claim has been denied. This brings concerned local authorities into direct conflict with this legislation as local authorities have a duty to act in the best interests of children, which is in clear conflict with separation from their parents.

Social workers face many challenges in supporting asylum seekers; the key challenge is to enable their employing organisations, particularly local authorities, to take a more proactive role. Local authorities need support from central government so that resources can be focused on providing personalised services that ameliorate the destitution faced by asylum seekers. However, as SCIE (2010) observes, social work and social care services will not be able to meet the needs of asylum seekers on their own as this requires a coordinated effort from many organisations. The needs of asylum seekers are complex in requiring a mix of practical, legal and emotional support to enable their human rights to be achieved. This means early assessment of need when the asylum process begins, coupled with the appropriate delivery of adults and children's services; this also means maintaining levels of service and intervention when asylum seekers move from one area to another as a result of the dispersal process.

Human trafficking and forced labour

The causes of trafficking lie in a range of socio-economic conditions that include poverty, poor employment opportunities, psychological vulnerability and discrimination. Singularly, or a combination of these factors, may force an individual to seek better opportunities through migration. These factors make migrants vulnerable to exploitation during the migration process, which is disproportionately overlaid with gender discrimination, making women and girls more vulnerable still. The vulnerability of women and girls (including once they arrive in the destination country) to this process is reinforced by a number of interlinking factors:

• lack of educational opportunity
• a higher proportion of women in informal and unprotected labour markets
• an unequal burden of caring for children and ageing relatives
• high levels of gender-based violence.

In the UK the changing nature of the population as it ages, coupled with gaps in the labour market, particularly in the 'caring industries', has provided opportunities for unscrupulous employers to exploit migrants. Cheaper and easier travel and the expansion of poorly regulated recruitment agencies enables the further exploitation of this group.

The number of people trafficked into the UK is hard to calculate, but between 1 April 2009 and 30 June 2011, 1,664 potential trafficked people were referred to the UK's formal identification process. Of these, 565 were formally recognised as trafficked. Over two thirds of referrals were women. Children made up 438 (26 per cent) of all referrals and 160 of those were formally recognised as trafficked.

Social workers working in the UK observing economic and forced migration within the context of globalisation need to understand the role played by immigration status in promoting international migrants' vulnerability to forced labour.

In the introduction to this chapter it was identified that the increasing economic pressure on nation states may compromise their national economic sovereignty because of the wider global economic forces bearing down on them. Nation states still retain much power and control in determining who crosses their borders, and these often restrictive policies have serious implications in respect of migrants' rights within a host country. There is a varied mix of rights to residence, work and access to welfare services attached to different types of migrants (dependent on their particular immigration status). This means that there is a stratified system of socio-legal entitlement that exists within the general population of migrants resident in the UK (Dwyer et al, 2011). Social workers therefore need to understand how different entitlements limit the access to services that may potentially meet migrants' needs. Likewise, the nature of low-paid employment with poor working conditions that many migrants experience reinforces the oppression of migrants and may make them more susceptible to forced labour.

'Human trafficking' is used to describe any activity where one person obtains or holds another person in compelled service. In effect, this is a modern form of enslavement, usually as a result of people being moved from one country to another, but not always. This exploitation can take many forms:

- the prostitution of others or other forms of sexual exploitation
- forced labour services
- slavery or practices similar to slavery
- servitude or the removal of organs.

Globally, the International Labour Organization (ILO, 2012) estimate that of the total number of 20.9 million forced labourers, 18.7 million (90 per cent) are exploited in the private economy by individuals or enterprises; out of these, 4.5 million (22 per cent) are victims of forced sexual exploitation, 14.2 million (68 per cent) are victims of forced labour exploitation in economic activities, such as agriculture, construction, domestic work or manufacturing, and 2.2 million (10 per cent) are in state-imposed forms of forced labour, for example, in prisons, or in work imposed by the state military or by rebel armed forces.

People are trafficked into the UK from a variety of countries; they are trafficked into the sex industry or smuggled into the UK to provide other forms of labour. The nature of trafficking as mentioned earlier has a clear gender bias. Many young women from Eastern Europe have been trafficked into the UK to feed the sex industry; this process has been given further momentum by the opening up of the European Community in 2004 to countries from Eastern Europe. The promise of a better lifestyle and an adequate livelihood links these disparate groups as the promise of legitimate work is revealed as a sham (Lyons et al, 2006). Those who are trafficked may therefore be deceived into their slavery with the offer of a job or position that will remove them from the extreme levels of poverty experienced by them in their own countries.

The UK is a major focus for the trafficking of people into the sex trade. Sex trafficking can result in large profits for those traffickers, as one woman can earn up to £1,000 per week for her trafficker. Women are kept in abject conditions and experience physical violence, drugging and imprisonment. Many live under constant fear from their traffickers, yet if they manage to escape, the UK immigration system puts them at risk of deportation. In turn, this creates the risk of those women being re-trafficked or shunned by their families when they return home, particularly if their families sold them in the first place.

If these women escape, they generally don't testify against their traffickers for fear of what might happen to their families at home, and in addition they may be deemed illegal immigrants. Unless help is provided at this stage they will not necessarily be recognised as victims of exploitation (House of Commons Home Affairs Committee, 2009). This was recognised by the Organization for Security and Co-operation in Europe (OSCE) (2011) in their assessment of UK policy; they saw the discrepancy between the number of referrals made to the Home Office and the number of victims who receive positive conclusive grounds for decisions to remain. The policy to date takes a criminal justice approach that does not address the needs and social contexts of the victims coming forward. A more holistic approach grounded in human rights, ensuring the right to protection, assistance and redress, will therefore encourage more victims to come forward and also increase the number of investigations and prosecutions. Social workers working in this area therefore need to take a less parochial view in combating trafficking. Thus any anti-trafficking initiatives need to address the social and economic conditions that underpin human trafficking. The Inter-Departmental Ministerial Group on Human Trafficking (2012) argues that working on the socio-economic conditions within the countries where migrants move from should reduce victims' vulnerability to trafficking, alongside improving the human rights of women in these countries. There are a number of organisations in the UK that social workers can refer any possible clients to, including the Hear programme, which supports trafficked women into, for example, higher education, the POPPY Project and Kalayaan, which provides English classes for their service users and offers support to enable them to enter the labour market.

Practice issues

Working within a punitive legislative system highlights the dilemmas faced by social workers wishing to alleviate the poverty that asylum seekers and trafficked people experience. Wright (2012) highlights these issues in relation to unaccompanied asylum-seeking children in identifying the constraints that result in the social work role being highly transcribed by the limits to which social workers can work outside the legal process of returning children to their countries of origin. Since 2010, Wright (2012) observes that social workers have noticed a significant change in policy from the Home Office. Many asylum-seeking young people, once they reach their 18th birthday, are refused permission to stay in the UK. The product of this policy, as Wright recognises, is that many young people, when faced with either a forced or voluntary return home, decide to abscond. To avoid young people and adults who choose this option from being more at risk, it is vital that they are put into contact with voluntary groups that can support them. Although social workers cannot condone breaking the law, they do have an ethical duty to discuss options with those who may be thinking of absconding. Therefore those refugee groups and voluntary organisations that have contact with refugee and asylum communities should be linked with the person considering such a desperate act. The majority of such organisations are usually staffed by people who may have experienced the same dilemmas as the absconding person, and are therefore in the best position to provide support. Dunkerley et al (2005), in their study of asylum in Wales, suggest that social workers often use their discretion to turn a blind eye to absconding behaviour. The use of such 'non-intervention' could involve seeking to support the individual/family outside of the system by using informal social networks or by involving voluntary campaigning groups, for example, in the case of children, Barnardo's, to take up the cases of children of failed asylum seekers.

> On the face of it, the comprehensive National Asylum Support Service regulations allow little room for discretion on the part of practitioners, and yet, as indicated above, the large majority of failed asylum-seekers are not removed from the country. In part, this must arise from professionals "turning a blind eye" or by not actively pursuing such individuals according to the letter of the law. The research reported here provides at least some indication of such practices. (Dunkerley et al, 2005, p 649)

Migrant labour and global care

Since 2004, when the EU expanded to include countries from Eastern Europe, over 800,000 migrants have registered with the Home Office to work in the UK, with the majority, 60 per cent, coming from Poland. Data collected in 2011 show there were estimated to be over 1.5 million registered foreign workers in the UK (Wilkinson, 2012). The legal status of migrant workers is highly complex, with many restrictions on their legal entitlement to work, and a highly complex system of visas and work permits that vary for different categories of workers and countries of origin. As a result, many migrant workers are unaware of their rights. In essence, the field of labour relations in this area is highly unregulated, with very little enforcement of standards (Oxfam, 2009). On arrival to the UK many migrant workers find themselves already in debt. They are usually required to pay an agency a signing on fee of up to £1,000 that in turn may pass them on to another agent who can charge a similar fee. Gangmasters may pay the minimum wage but then make a number of charges for transport to work and for clothing, charges that are illegal. The UK currently has more temporary workers than any other country in Europe as the poor regulatory framework has attracted innumerable employment agencies and unscrupulous gangmasters; a recent estimate in 2006 suggested there were up to 10,000 gangmasters operating in the UK (House of Commons Home Affairs Committee, 2009).

Although in this section we focus on those workers employed in the care sector, migrant labour covers a wider range of occupations, including farm work, domestic service and the hotel and restaurant trade. In relation to care work, again, the focus is on social care, which forms part of a globalised care sector (Yeates, 2012) encompassing intimate social care and health services such as cooking, cleaning, ironing and general maintenance work. As such this is a highly gendered sphere, and reproduces many of the unequal gendered social relations found in the 'mainstream' economy.

Migrant workers are seen as very attractive propositions for employers, bringing advantages in terms of cheaper labour costs and increased flexibility, for example, in that many migrant workers are prepared to work unsocial hours. Given the ambiguity and lack of workers' rights, unscrupulous employers clearly see many benefits in exploiting such labour. This exploitation is often reinforced by actions of the states that migrant workers travel from, given the remittances that they send back to their home country and the wider requirements to maintain free trade.

Migrant care workers are in an impossible situation unless a more effective means of organising to improve their status at work can be found. Any attempts to organise must understand the constraints on such workers to 'accept' low wages and poor conditions, with many workers depending on their employers to renew their legal immigration status. Migrants, by nature of their position, are in a state of insecurity as they may have temporary rights (for example, work permit holders) or have no legal rights (for example, people who have overstayed entry visas) to work and remain in the UK. These insecurities clearly shape their relations with employers, including experiences of wages being withheld and overtime being unpaid (Shutes, 2012).

The advantages of a migrant care force servicing such areas as home-based care and residential care within the social services sector are clear in terms of the UK government's programme of cost containment and restructuring of the welfare state. Shutes (2012, p 101) identified that:

> ... the percentage of foreign-born care workers (care assistants and home carers) in the UK more than doubled over the last decade, from 7% of care workers in 2001 to 18% in 2009.

Higher concentrations of migrant care labour can be found in the major cities, with London having 51 per cent of its care force supplied by non-UK citizens.

Social workers need to understand the experiences of care workers in terms of their perilous position, who are, in effect, living below the poverty line and yet are expected to care for differently vulnerable people. Paradoxically, new migrant workers in the care sector are significantly younger and hold higher qualifications relevant to social care; interestingly, no significant gender differences have been found within the new arrivals group (Hussein et al, 2011).

Manthorpe et al (2012), in their research, have charted where care staff had difficulties communicating with relatives and people using care services, therefore compromising the quality of care. They argue that social workers need to be alert to the risks facing service users, carers and migrant care workers in such contexts. Both service users and migrant workers occupy different marginalised spaces where their relative lack of power and impoverishment is reflected in these micro encounters of care. In effect, as Shutes and Chiatti (2012) argue in the context of residential and home care services in England, the costs of care have been shifted onto low-waged migrant workers employed by publicly and privately contracted service providers.

> While "non-migrant", citizen workers, predominantly women, continue to make up the majority of workers in care services overall, migrant labour has supplemented that labour to a greater extent within the private sector, for relatively lower wages and under worse employment conditions. (Shutes and Chiatti, 2012, p 401)

Summary

The challenge social workers face in working with asylum seekers, migrant workers and trafficked people goes beyond the confines of the local area offices to which local authority social workers and their colleagues in the voluntary sector work. The diverse nature of these problems therefore sits at the global level, highlighting how social problems are interrelated between different countries across the globe (Yeates, 2012). In turn, the interrelatedness of such problems requires social workers looking beyond the borders of their own country to work with social workers from countries where, for example, people seek asylum or who are trafficked from. International social work of this kind requires employers and social workers being more expansive in looking beyond the parochial nature of social work as it has been practised. This requires engaging with others from other countries around those practice issues that they share in common in order to build new insights and ways of working to combat the abuses that people are subject to, as described in this chapter. In a globalised world poverty does discriminate; it is overwhelmingly experienced by those people in countries seen as less 'developed' economically than the rich West. Nevertheless, the problems associated with asylum seekers and trafficked people are not rooted in one country. As Ahmadi (2003) argues, developing an international dimension to social work has the potential for setting new practice standards to combat abuse, poverty and discrimination worldwide. It must emphasise the global values of human rights and work towards their implementation across the globe. Thus practice needs to renew its focus from a concern solely with poverty in the specific countries in which social workers practice, towards an international dimension that charts the global effects of neo-liberal policies as they have an effect on social relations between and within different countries.

This chapter has identified the impact of globalisation on the social and economic policies of nation states. It has focused on three aspects of globalisation in relation to social work: that of asylum seekers, migrant workers and those trafficked into the UK. It has identified the implications of the UK government's response to these issues as creating destitution for people seeking asylum and the impact this then has on their lives. It has argued for a social work response that deals at first hand with the problems of destitution and homelessness that confronts asylum seekers and those trafficked, as well as thinking beyond the confines of national boundaries. In so doing it has argued for a globalised response from social work to the challenges of poverty and destitution that have their genesis beyond the borders of the UK.

Recommended reading

Farnsworth, K. (2012) *Social versus corporate welfare: Competing needs and interests within the welfare state*, London: Palgrave.

Lyons, K., Manion, K. and Carlsen, M. (2006) *International perspectives on social work: Global conditions and local practice*, Basingstoke: Palgrave.

Conclusion

We began this book by placing social work and its engagement with poverty in a historical context. We identified the way in which the early pioneers in social work, such as the COS, were concerned to maintain a clear distinction between those who 'deserved' to be helped and those considered too 'feckless' to benefit from the casework of the COS. This distinction between the deserving and undeserving resounds to this day in the way that the current Coalition government has constructed its welfare reform policies. As identified in the WRA 2012, policies such as 'the benefit cap' reflect attitudes of desert. Those in receipt of Working Tax Credit are exempted from the cap, as are those seen as deserving in other ways, for example, if a household is receiving a benefit related to disability or a war widows benefit (DWP, 2013a). Thus, only those who are seen as looking for work, that is, the able-bodied poor, are subject to a policy of less eligibility. Those able-bodied poor who are made redundant or who live in an area of high unemployment, through no fault of their own, are punished. I work close to the industrial town of Stoke-on-Trent, which has one of the highest rates of people claiming Jobseeker's Allowance in the country. The ratio of unemployed people to jobs available in the area is one of the worst in England, with 12 jobseekers for every one vacancy available; the worst place is Hull, with 53 jobseekers for every one vacancy (Office for National Statistics, 2013). To highlight this in a less academic way, all the national newspapers recently reported that 1,701 people had applied for eight jobs working for Costa Coffee in their new Nottingham branch (*The Independent*, 2013).

It is likely that the impact of the WRA 2012 will further impoverish many service users that social workers come into contact with. It is my view that the extent of poverty will mean that, for the first time perhaps since the 1930s, many people claiming social security will experience levels of absolute poverty that we thought would never return. Early assessments of the impact of welfare reform have identified the significant effect the loss of incomes will have on communities. Beatty and Fothergill (2013) estimate that some £19 billion will be taken out of the economy in England; in terms of its specific impact, the three regions of northern England will lose £5.2 billion. These figures represent serious loses of income for poorer communities. On an individual basis, depending on which group of claimants we are looking at, people will be losing significant amounts of money; for example, a single parent claiming Jobseeker's Allowance and living in London stands to lose up to £93 a week as a result of cumulative changes to Housing Benefit and the overall benefits cap (Channel 4, 2013).

Social workers need to be very clear that they do not operate within this mindset of only helping those who they think 'deserve' such help. They need to be aware that the Coalition government, in my view, is working within this mindset, of dividing those in work from those on benefit, to justify the cuts they are implementing. As this book has identified, service users who live in poverty experience the daily injustice and stigma of having their motives questioned as to why they are claimants. Working within this undeserving paradigm creates fear and hostility that prevents social workers from effectively engaging with service users. The argument in this book is that to work in an anti-oppressive way with service users experiencing poverty requires social workers working at a number of levels.

In working to combat poverty, social workers need to focus their attention on three levels:

• individual
• organisational
• social.

Each of these levels is interrelated, and therefore changes in one level will have implications for another. For example, we have seen how at the social level the Coalition government has instituted profound changes to the social security system in response to the immediate shock of the global banking crisis and the ongoing requirement, as they argue, to enable the UK to compete in global markets. This concern to attract foreign investment focuses on reducing the level of social costs to make the UK more attractive for foreign global capital to invest. One of the effects of such policies has been for social workers to come into contact with people from other countries seeking work or asylum living in severe poverty or in fear of being deported back to their country of origin. At the organisational level, particularly within local authorities, social workers experience the way in which their employing organisations have outsourced the provision of social services so that their role has become more focused on managing access to these services rather than providing them. Consequently, social workers' practice has become increasingly tied to fulfilling managerial procedures that limit their professional judgement. Social workers in children and families teams deal solely with concerns of child protection, with preventative work hived off to outside agencies, so limiting the time they may have to address issues of poverty. At the individual level, service users who are claimants are required to be constantly work-focused in order to remove themselves as quickly as possible from the claimant count.

How should social workers respond? Just as the effects of poverty operate at a number of levels, social workers need a repertoire of responses to effectively engage with the poverty of service users. This book has outlined that at the individual level, social workers' intervention has to focus on both the emotional impacts that experiencing poverty has for individuals as well as the material deprivations. Social workers therefore need to provide empathic support for service users and be aware of the ongoing stresses that occur when individuals and families struggle with the effects of poverty. This requires social workers to maximise the incomes of service users. As this book has shown, opportunities to maximise incomes from social security benefit is becoming harder, but this should not deter social workers from exploring any valid options, through involving welfare rights and other advice workers in attempting to increase the incomes of service users, however small the increases might be. Even the addition of a few pounds a week can make a difference to the lives of service users.

At the organisational level, social workers need to be aware of their power to exercise their discretion in helping service users to access resources available from within the wider net of social services. They need to join with their colleagues in working within their organisations to become more poverty-aware and to have this awareness reflected in the policies and procedures by which the organisation manages service delivery. To improve poverty awareness within organisations, a poverty audit could be instigated that would assess policies and procedures in the light of whether they contribute or seek to alleviate poverty; similar audits have been used in the US in relation to ethical practice (Reamer, 2005).

Social workers are more effective when they work together, and this can be achieved within different forums. Professional associations such as the British Association of Social Workers (BASW) can provide a professional voice, both locally and at national level, in bringing the issue of poverty centre stage in social work. The Social Work Action Network (SWAN) (2013) also provides an alternative voice that has campaigned successfully around a number of issues that have direct relevance for service users experiencing poverty. Involvement in a trade union such as UNISON, the main union representative of social workers, can provide links to the wider community of workers within a locality, and at national level, many trade unions, particularly UNISON, have been vocal in mounting campaigns opposing the WRA 2012 and the privatisation of social work services (see UNISON, 2008). Social workers working alongside service user groups at a local and national level can help bring people living in poverty into the policy and service delivery process to effect change. At a wider social level, social workers may want to be involved in a campaigning group such as CPAG and/or a political party that is genuinely seeking to improve the conditions of service users.

There is recognition that social work needs to return to working more closely with communities through a community social work orientation that has, until now, been slowly eroded over the past 30 years. Mantle and Backwith (2010) argue for a community-oriented social work in combating poverty which is involved in finding practical solutions to the problems that individuals and communities face; for example, developing Credit Unions to provide credit to those financially excluded by the lending banks or those further financially exploited by loan companies. Ultimately they call for an invigoration of the radical alternative in social work that has formed such a significant part of the history of social work practice, particularly since the late 1960s. As such this involves a continuing and ongoing commitment to AOP, explored in some detail in this book.

In the Introduction to this book I voiced the hope that people reading this would feel angry enough to want to campaign and to actively become involved in seeking to end poverty in the UK. Although social work of itself will never abolish poverty (at best it can only modify some of the harsher consequences for service users), social workers working alongside service users and others in the wider community can create a groundswell of opposition to oppose the continuing immiseration and impoverishment of us all.

Recommended reading

Ferguson, I., Lavallette, M. and Mooney, G. (2002) *Rethinking welfare: A critical approach*, London: Sage Publications.

Mantle, G. and Backwith, D. (2010) 'Poverty and social work', *British Journal of Social Work*, vol 40, pp 2380-97.

References

Adams, R. (2003) *Social work and empowerment*, Basingstoke: Palgrave.

Adelman, L., Middleton, S. and Ashworth, K. (2003) *Britain's poorest children: Severe and persistent poverty and social exclusion*, London: Save the Children.

Age UK (2012) 'Factsheet 46: Paying for care and support at home' (www.ageuk. org.uk/GB/Factsheets/FS46.pdf).

Ahmadi, N. (2003) 'Globalisation of consciousness and new challenges for international social work', *International Journal of Social Welfare*, vol 12, pp 14-23.

Alcock, P. (2006) *Understanding poverty*, Basingstoke: Palgrave.

Aldridge, H., Kenway, P., MacInnes, T. and Parekh, A. (2012) *Monitoring poverty and social exclusion*, York: Joseph Rowntree Trust.

Aldridge, H. and Tinson, A. (2013) *How many families are affected by more than one benefit cut this April?* London: New Policy Institute.

Allan, J. (2006) 'Whose job is poverty? The problems of therapeutic intervention with children who are sexually violent', *Child Abuse Review*, vol 15, pp 55-70.

Anand, P. and Lea, S. (2011) 'The psychology and behavioural economics of poverty', *Journal of Economic Psychology*, no 32, pp 284-93.

Athwal, B., Quiggin, M., Phillips, D. and Harrison, M. (2011) *Exploring experiences of poverty in Bradford*, York: Joseph Rowntree Trust.

Audit Commission (2012) *Learning from inspection: Housing Benefit administration*, London: Audit Commission.

Bacchetta, M. and Jansen, M. (2011) *Making globalisation socially sustainable*, Geneva: World Trade Organization.

Bailey, K. (2012) 'Policy based on unethical research', Poverty and Social Exclusion (www.poverty.ac.uk/news-and-views/articles/policy-built-unethical-research).

Barn, R. (2007) 'Race, ethnicity and parenting: Understanding the impact of context', *Childright*, no 233, pp 24-7.

Barnard, M. (2005) *Drugs in the family: The impact on parents and siblings*, York: Joseph Rowntree Trust.

Bartlett, A. and Preston, D. (2000) 'Can ethical behaviour really exist in business?', *Journal of Business Ethics*, vol 3, no 2, pp 199-215.

Bauman, Z. (1994) *Alone again: Ethics after certainty*, London: Demos.

Bauman, Z. (2005) *Work, consumerism and the new poor*, Buckingham: Open University Press.

Beatty, C. and Fothergill, N. (2013) *Hitting the poorest places hardest: The local and regional impact of welfare reform*, Sheffield: Sheffield Hallam University (www. shu.ac.uk/mediacentre/first-evidence-overall-impact-welfare-reform-across-britain).

Bebbington, P., Jonas, S., Brugha, T., Meltzer, H., Jenkins, R., Cooper, C., King, M. and McManus, S. (2011) 'Child sexual abuse reported by an English national sample: characteristics and demography', *Social Psychiatry and Psychiatric Epidemiology*, vol 46, no 3, pp 255-69.

Becker, S. (1997) *Responding to poverty: The politics of cash and care*, London: Longman.

Beresford, P., Green, D., Lister, R. and Woodward, K. (1999) *Poverty first hand: Poor people speak for themselves*, London: Child Poverty Action Group.

Bowers, H., Clark, C., Crosby, G., Easterbrook, L., Macadam, A., MacDonald, R., Macfarlane, A., Maclean, M., Patel, M., Runnicles, D., Oshinaike, T. and Smith, C. (2009) *Older people's vision for long-term care*, York: Joseph Rowntree Foundation.

Bradshaw, J. (ed) (1993) *Budget standards for the United Kingdom*, Aldershot: Avebury.

Bradshaw, J., Middleton, S., Davis, A., Oldfield, N., Smith, N., Cusworth, L. and Williams, J. (2008) *A minimum income standard for Britain: What people think*, York: Joseph Rowntree Trust.

Brewer, M., Browne, J. and Jin, W. (2012) 'Universal Credit: A preliminary analysis of its impact on incomes and work incentives', *Fiscal Studies*, vol 33, no 1, pp 39-71.

Brewer, M., Browne, J. and Joyce, R. (2011) *Child and working age poverty 2010-2020*, York: Joseph Rowntree Foundation.

British Medical Journal (2010) 'Childhood protection and obesity: framework for practice', (http://dx.doi.org/10.1136/bmj.c3074).

Broadhurst, K., Wastell, D., White, S., Hall, C., Peckover, S., Thompson, K., Pithouse, A. and Dolores, D. (2009) 'Performing "initial assessments": Identifying the latent conditions for error at the front-door of local authority children's services', *British Journal of Social Work*, Vol 40, no 2, pp 352-370.

Brown, J. (1973) 'Drink and poverty in late Victorian Britain', *International Review of Social History*, vol 18, pp 380-95.

Brundage, A. (2002) *The English Poor Laws 1700-1930*, Basingstoke: Palgrave.

Brutscher, P. (2011) *Self-disconnection among pre-payment customers – A behavioural analysis*, EPRG Working Paper 1207, Cambridge Working Paper in Economics 1214, Cambridge: University of Cambridge.

Buchanan, J. (2004) 'Missing Links: Problem Drug Use and Social Exclusion', *Probation Journal Special Edition on Problem Drug Use*, Vol 51, no 4 pp 387-397.

Buchanan, J. (2010) 'Drug policy under New Labour 1997-2010: Prolonging the war on drugs', *Probation Journal*, vol 57, no 3, pp 250-62.

Buchanan, J. and Corby, B. (2005) 'Problem drug use: A new conceptual framework', in R. Carnwell and J. Buchanan (eds) *Effective practice in health and social care: A partnership approach*, Maidenhead: Open University Press, pp 163-79.

CAB (Citizens' Advice Bureau) (2013) *Measuring child poverty: A consultation on better measures of child poverty: Response by Citizens Advice*, London: CAB.

Cameron, D. (2006) 'The challenges of globalisation', Speech given on 5 September, London, Conservative Party.

Cameron, D. (2011) 'Troubled families speech' (www.number10.gov.uk/news/troubled–families–speech).

Cancian, M., Shook Slack, K. and Youn Yang, M. (2010) *The effect of family income on risk of child maltreatment*, Institute for Research on Poverty Discussion Paper no 1385-1, Wisconsin, Madison, WI: School of Social Work and Institute for Research on Poverty, University of Wisconsin-Madison.

Centre for Policy on Ageing (2008) *Ageism and age discrimination in social care in the United Kingdom: A review from the literature*, London: Centre for Policy on Ageing/Department of Health.

Chambon, A., Irving, A. and Epstein, L. (eds) (1999) *Reading Foucault for social work*, New York: Columbia University Press.

Channel 4 (2013) 'Families consider options as benefit cap begins', 15 April (www.channel4.com/news/benefits-cap-london-iain-duncan-smith-housing-benefit-begin).

Chantarat, S. and Barrett, C. (2011) 'Social network capital, economic mobility and poverty traps', *Journal of Economic Inequality*, Online, 18 February, pp 1-44 (https://researchers.anu.edu.au/publications/58783).

Charlesworth, L. (2001) 'The poet and the Poor Law. Reflections upon John Clare's "The parish"', *Liverpool Law Review*, no 23, pp 167-78.

Children's Society, The (2012) *Highlighting the gap between asylum support and mainstream benefits*, London: The Children's Society.

Cleaver, H., Unell, I. and Aldgate, J. (2011) *Children's needs – Parenting capacity – Child abuse: Parental mental illness, learning disability, substance misuse and domestic violence*, Norwich: The Stationery Office.

Clough, R., Manthorpe, J., Raymond, V., Sumner, K., Bright, L., Hay, J., OPRSI (Older People Researching Social Issues), Joseph Rowntree Foundation and Eskrigge Social Research (2007) *The support older people want and the services they need*, York: Joseph Rowntree Foundation.

Coalition on Charging (2008) *Charging into poverty: Challenging charges* (www.disabilityalliance.org/chargingintopoverty.pdf).

Colby, S., Paulson, M., Johnson, L. and Wall-Bassett, E. (2010) 'Reaching North Dakota's Food Insecure', *Journal of Hunger & Environmental Nutrition*, vol 5, no 1, pp 129-35.

Coleman, N. and Harris, J. (2008) 'Calling social work', *British Journal of Social Work*, vol 38, no 3, pp 580-99.

Contact a Family (2011) *Forgotten families: The impact of isolation on families with disabled children across the UK 2011* (www.cafamily.org.uk/media/381636/forgotten_isolation_report.pdf).

Contact a Family (2012) *Counting the costs: The financial reality for families with disabled children across the UK* (www.cafamily.org.uk/media/381221/counting_the_costs_2012_full_report.pdf).

Counsel and Care (2008) *Care contradictions: Putting people first? The harsh reality for older people, their families and carers of increasing charges and tightening criteria*, London: Counsel and Care.

CPAG (Child Poverty Action Group) (2012) *Universal Credit: What you need to know*, London: CPAG.

CQC (Care Quality Commission) (2011a) *The state of social care in England 2009-10*, London: CQC.

CQC (2011b) *Dignity and nutrition inspection programme: National overview*, London: CQC.

Crawley, H. (2010) *Chance or choice? Understanding why asylum seekers come to the UK*, London: Refugee Council.

Cribb, J., Joyce, R. and Phillips, D. (2012) *Living standards, poverty and inequality in the UK: 2012*, London: Institute for Fiscal Studies.

Crouch, C. (2003) *Commercialisation or citizenship: Education policy and the future of public services*, Fabian Ideas No 506, London: Fabian Society.

Crowley, A. and Vulliamy, C. (2011) *Listen up! Children and young people talk about poverty*, Cardiff: Save the Children.

Daguerre, A. and Etherington, D. (2009) *Active labour market policies in international context: What works best? Lessons for the UK*, DWP Working Paper No 59, London: The Stationery Office.

Daily Mail (2013) 'Vile product of Welfare UK', 3 April (www.dailymail.co.uk/news/article-2303120/Mick-Philpott-vile-product-Welfare-UK-Derby-man-bred-17-babies-milk-benefits-GUILTY-killing-six.html).

Daily Telegraph (2012a) 'Speech by Prime Minister David Cameron on welfare reform', Bluewater, Kent, 25 June.

Daily Telegraph (2012b) 'Problem families "have too many children": Mothers in large problem families should be "ashamed" of the damage they are doing to society and stop having children, a senior Government adviser warns today', 20 July (www.telegraph.co.uk/news/politics/9416535/Problem-families-have-too-many-children.html).

Daily Telegraph (2013) 'Iain Duncan Smith: I could live on £53 per week', 1 April (www.telegraph.co.uk/news/politics/9964767/Iain-Duncan-Smith-I-could-live-on-53-per-week.html).

David, G. (2012) 'The WCA independent review: Fit for purpose?', 3 December (http://wheresthebenefit.blogspot.co.uk/2010/12/wca-independent-review-fit-for-purpose.html).

Davies, M. (2008) *Eradicating child poverty: The role of key policy areas: The effects of discrimination on families in the fight to end child poverty*, York: Joseph Rowntree Foundation.

Davis, A. and Wainwright, S. (2005) 'Combating poverty and social exclusion: Implications for social work education', *Social Work Education*, vol 24, no 3, pp 259-73.

Davis, A., Hirsch, D., Smith, N., Beckhelling, J. and Padley, M. (2012) *A minimum income standard for the UK in 2012*, York: Joseph Rowntree Trust.

DCLG (Department for Communities and Local Government) (2012) *Listening to troubled families*, London: DCLG.

Dean, H. (2002) *Welfare rights and social policy*, Harlow: Pearson Press.

Dean, H. (2010) *Understanding human need*, Bristol: Policy Press.

DECC (Department of Energy and Climate Change) (2012) *Annual report on fuel poverty statistics 2012*, London: National Statistics Publication.

DEFRA (Department of the Environment, Food and Rural Affairs) (2011) *Family food*, www.gov.uk/government/publications/family-food-2011

DfE (Department for Education) (2012) *Statistical release: Children looked after in England: Year ending 31st March*, SFR 20/2012, London: DfE.

DfES (Department for Education and Science) (2002) *Children Act report 2002*, London: The Stationery Office.

Department for Education and Skills (2004) *Every child matters: Change for children in social care*, London, DfES.

DH (Department of Health) (2009) *Valuing people now: A new three-year strategy for people with learning disabilities, 'Making it happen for everyone'*, London: The Stationery Office.

DH (2102) *Caring for our future: Reforming care and support*, Cm 8378, London: The Stationery Office.

Dorey, P. (2010) 'A poverty of imagination: Blaming the poor for inequality', *Political Quarterly*, vol 83, no 3, pp 333-46.

Dowler, E. (2003) 'Food and poverty: Insights from the "North"', *Development Policy Review*, vol 21, no 5-6, pp 569-80.

Dowler, E. and O'Connor, D. (2012) 'Rights-based approaches to addressing food poverty and food insecurity in Ireland and UK', *Social Science & Medicine*, vol 74, pp 44-51.

Dowling, M. (1999) *Social work and poverty*, Aldershot: Ashgate.

Dunkerley, D., Scourfield, J., Maegusuku-Hewett, T. and Smalley, N. (2005) 'The experiences of front-line staff working with children, seeking asylum', *Social Policy & Administration*, vol 39, no 6, pp 640-52.

Dustin, D. (2007) *The McDonaldisation of social work*, Aldershot: Ashgate.

DWP (2010a) *Housing Benefit: Changes to the local housing allowance arrangements*, DWP Impact Assessment, 24 November.

DWP (2010b) *21st century welfare*, The Stationery Office, London.

DWP (2010c) *Universal Credit: Welfare that works*, The Stationery Office, London.

DWP (2011) *A new approach to child poverty: Tackling the causes of disadvantage and transforming families' lives*, Cm 8061, London: The Stationery Office.

DWP (2012a) *Measuring child poverty: A consultation on better measures of child poverty*, London: The Stationery Office.

DWP (2012b) *Social justice: Transforming lives*, Cm 8314, London: The Stationery Office.

DWP (2012c) *Housing Benefit: Under occupation of social housing*, Impact Assessment, 28 June.

DWP (2013a) 'Benefit cap factsheet', www.dwp.gov.uk/docs/benefit-cap-factsheet.pdf

DWP (2013b) 'Hoban taking action to improve the Work Capability Assessment', press release 22 July, www.gov.uk/government/news/hoban-taking-action-to-improve-the-work-capability-assessment.

Dwyer, P., Lewis, H., Scullion, L. and Waite, L. (2011) *Forced labour and UK immigration policy: Status matters?*, York: Joseph Rowntree Trust.

EHRC (Equalities and Human Rights Commission) (2011) *Close to home: An inquiry into older people and human rights in home care* (www.equalityhumanrights.com/uploaded_files/homecareFI/home_care_report.pdf).

Eichhorst, W. and Konle-Seidl, R. (2008) *Contingent convergence: A comparative analysis of activation policies*, Intensive Econometric Research IZA DP No 3905, Bonn: Institute for the Study of Labor (IZA).

Ellis, K. (2007) 'Direct payments and social work practice: The significance of "street-level bureaucracy" in determining eligibility', *British Journal of Social Work*, vol 37, pp 405-22.

Emerson, E. and Hatton, C. (2007) *The mental health of children and adolescents with learning disabilities in Britain*, London: Foundation for People with Learning Disabilities.

Englander, D. (1998) *Poverty and Poor Law reform in 19th century Britain, 1834-1914: From Chadwick to Booth*, London: Longman.

Evans, T. (2011) 'Professionals, managers and discretion: Critiquing street-level bureaucracy', *British Journal of Social Work*, vol 41, pp 368-86.

Evans, T. and Harris, J. (2004) 'Street level bureaucracy, social work and the (exaggerated) death of discretion', *British Journal of Social Work*, vol 34, no 6, pp 871-95.

Farnsworth, K. (2012) *Social versus corporate welfare: Competing needs and interests within the welfare state*, London: Palgrave.

Farnsworth, K. and Holden, C. (2006) 'The business-social policy nexus: Corporate power and corporate inputs into social policy', *Journal of Social Policy*, vol 35, no 3, pp 473-94.

Fenton, A. (2010) *Which neighbourhoods in London will be affordable for Housing Benefit claimants 2010-16, as the government's reforms take effect?*, Cambridge: Centre for Housing and Planning Research, University of Cambridge/Shelter (www.shelter.org.uk/__data/assets/pdf_file/0018/300906/Summary_of_London_housing_benefit_affordability_map.pdf).

Ferguson, I. and Woodward, R. (2009) *Radical social work in practice: Making a difference*, Bristol: Policy Press.

Ferguson, I., Lavallette, M. and Mooney, G. (2002) *Rethinking welfare: A critical approach*, London: Sage Publications.

Fielder, P. (2006) *Social welfare in pre-industrial England*, Basingstoke: Palgrave.

Fook, J. (2012) *Social work: A critical approach to practice*, London: Sage Publications.

Foresight Programme (2007) *Tackling obesities: Future choices – Project report*, October, UK Government Office for Science.

Freire, P. (1997) *Pedagogy of the oppressed* (2nd edn), New York: Continuum.

Frost, N. and Parton, N. (2009) *Understanding children's social care: Politics, policy and practice*, London: Sage Publications.

FSA (Food Standards Agency) (2007) *Safe food and healthy eating for all annual report 2007/2008* (www.official-documents.gov.uk/document/hc0708/hc08/0805/0805.pdf).

Galvani, S. and Hughes, N. (2010) 'Working with alcohol and drug use: Exploring the knowledge and attitudes of social work students', *British Journal of Social Work*, vol 40, pp 946-62.

Garrett, P. (2009) *Transforming children's services? Social work, neoliberalism and the 'modern' world*, Maidenhead: McGraw Hill/Open University Press.

Gillespie, M. (2012) *Destitution and asylum in Scotland,* Glasgow: Scottish Poverty Information Unit.

Gilligan, P. (2007) 'Well-motivated reformists or nascent radicals: How do applicants to the degree in social work see social problems, their origins and solutions?', *British Journal of Social Work*, vol 37, no 4, pp 735-60.

Gough, I. (1979) *The political economy of the welfare state*, London: Macmillan.

Gough, I. (2000) *Global capital, human needs and social policies*, Basingstoke: Palgrave.

Gould, N. (2006) *Mental health and child poverty*, York: Joseph Rowntree Trust.

Goulden, C. (2010) *Cycles of poverty, unemployment and low pay*, York: Joseph Rowntree Trust.

Gray, B. (2009) 'Befriending excluded families in Tower Hamlets: The emotional labour of family support workers in cases of child protection and family support', *British Journal of Social Work*, vol 39, pp 990-1007.

Green, J. (2009) 'The deformation of professional formation: Managerial targets and the undermining of professional judgement', *Ethics and Social Welfare*, vol 3, no 2, pp 115-30.

Green, M. (2007) *Voices of people experiencing poverty in Scotland: Everyone matters?*, York: Joseph Rowntree Trust.

Griggs, J. and Bennett, F. (2009) *Rights and responsibilities in the social security system*, Social Security Advisory Committee Occasional Paper No 6, London: Social Security Advisory Committee.

Grover, C. (2010) 'Social security policy and vindictiveness', *Sociological Research Online*, vol 15, no 2, p 8 (www.socresonline.org.uk/15/2/8.html).

Gupta, A. and Blewett, J. (2008) *Involving service users in social work training on the reality of family poverty: A case study of a collaborative project*, London: Social Care Workforce Research Unit, Kings College London.

Hankins, J. (2012) *ESA appeals* (www.nawra.org.uk/Documents/Cardiff_Mar_10/ ESA_appeals_Jackie_Hankins_Neath_Port_Talbot_WRS.pdf).

Hannon, C., Bazalgette, L. and Wood, C. (2010) *In loco parentis*, London: Demos.

Harkness, S., Gregg, P. and Macmillan, L. (2012) *Poverty: The role of institutions, behaviours and culture*, York: Joseph Rowntree Trust.

Harrington, M. (2010) *An independent review of the Work Capability Assessment – Year one*, London: The Stationery Office.

Harrington, M. (2011) *An independent review of the Work Capability Assessment – Year two*, London: The Stationery Office.

Harris, J. and White, V. (eds) (2009) *Modernising social work: Critical considerations*, Bristol: Policy Press.

Harvey, D. (2005) *A brief history of neoliberalism*, Oxford: Oxford University Press.

Harwin, J., Ryan, M. and Tunnard, J., with Pokhrel, S., Alrouh, B., Matias, C. and Momenian-Schneider, S. (2011) *The Family Drug and Alcohol Court (FDAC) evaluation project final report*, May, London: Brunel University.

Heffernan, K. (2006) 'Social work, new public management and the language of "service user"', *British Journal of Social Work*, no 36, pp 139-47.

Higgins, M. and Smith, W. (2002) 'Engaging the commodified face: the use of marketing in the child adoption process', *Business Ethics: A European Review*, vol 11, no 2, pp 179-90.

Hill, R. and Rapp, J. (2009) 'Globalization and poverty: Oxymoron or new possibilities?', *Journal of Business Ethics*, vol 85, pp 39-47.

Hills, J. (2012) *Getting the measure of fuel poverty: Final report of the Fuel Poverty Review*, London: Department of Energy and Climate Change.

Hirst, P., Thompson, G. and Bromley, S. (2009) *Globalization in question* (3rd edn), Cambridge: Polity Press.

HMRC (Her Majesty's Revenue & Customs) (2012) *Measuring the tax gaps*, London: HMRC.

Holben, D. (2013) 'Food Bank users in and around the Lower Mainland of British Columbia, Canada, are characterized by food insecurity and poor produce intake', *Journal of Hunger & Environmental Nutrition*, vol 7, no 4, pp 449-58.

Holford, A. (2012) *Take-up of free school meals: Price effects and peer effects*, Colchester: Institute for Social and Economic Research, University of Essex, Economic and Social Research Council.

Horvath, J. (2011) 'See the practitioner, see the child: The framework for the assessment of children in need and their families ten years on', *British Journal of Social Work*, vol 41, pp 1070-87.

House of Commons Education Select Committee (2012) *Education Committee – Fourth report, Children first: The child protection system in England* (www.publications.parliament.uk/pa/cm201213/cmselect/cmeduc/137/13702.htm).

House of Commons Health Committee (2004) *Obesity, Third report of Session 2003-04, Volume 1 report* (www.publications.parliament.uk/pa/cm200304/cmselect/cmhealth/23/23.pdf)

House of Commons Home Affairs Committee (2009) The trade in human beings: Human trafficking in the UK, Sixth report of Session 2008-09, London: The Stationery Office.

House of Commons Public Accounts Committee (2013) *Thirty-third report, Department for Work and Pensions: Work Programme outcome statistics* (www.parliament.uk/business/committees/committees-a-z/commons-select/public-accounts-committee).

House of Commons Work and Pensions Committee (2011) *The role of Incapacity Benefit reassessment in helping claimants into employment, Sixth report of Session 2010-12*, vol I (www.parliament.uk/workpencom).

Humphreys, C. (2007) 'A health inequalities perspective on violence against women', *Health & Social Care in the Community*, vol 15, no 2, pp 120-7.

Hussein, S., Manthorpe, J. and Stevens, M. (2011) 'Social care as first work experience in England: a secondary analysis of the profile of a national sample of migrant workers', *Health & Social Care in the Community*, vol 19, no 1, pp 89-97.

ILO (International Labour Organization) (2012) *Global estimate of forced labour: Executive summary* (www.ilo.org/wcmsp5/groups/public/@ed_norm/@declaration/documents/publication/wcms_181953.pdf).

Ince, D. and Griffiths, A. (2010) *A chronicling system for children's social work: Learning from the ICS failure*, Technical Report 2010/02, http://computing-reports.open.ac.uk/2010/TR2010-02.pdf

Independent, The (2013) 'More than 1,700 people apply for just EIGHT jobs at Costa Coffee shop', 13 February (www.independent.co.uk/news/uk/home-news/more-than-1700-people-apply-for-just-eight-jobs-at-costa-coffee-shop-8501329.html).

Inter-Departmental Ministerial Group on Human Trafficking (2012) *First annual report of the Inter-Departmental Ministerial Group on Human Trafficking*, London: The Stationery Office.

Institute of Education (2010) *Three in four Pakistani and Bangladeshi children in UK living in poverty at age 7*, London: Institute of Education.

Ipsos MORI (2011) *Trust in the professions: Trust and veracity survey* (www.ipsos-mori.com/Assets/Docs/Polls/ipsos-mori-trust-in-professions-june-2011-tables.pdf).

Jones, C. (1983) *State social work and the working class*, Basingstoke: Macmillan.

Jordan, B. (2007) *Social work and well-being*, Lyme Regis: Russell House.

Juby, C. and Meyer, E. (2010) 'Child nutrition policies and recommendations', *Journal of Social Work*, vol 11, no 4, pp 375-86.

Katz, I., Corlyon, J., La Placa, V. and Hunter, S. (2007) *The relationship between parenting and poverty*, York: Joseph Rowntree Trust.

Kidd, A. (1999) *State, society and the poor in nineteenth-century England*, Basingstoke: Macmillan.

Klee, H., McLean, I. and Yavorsky, C. (2002) *Services for people with drug problems seeking work*, York: Joseph Rowntree Trust.

Krumer-Nevo, M. (2005) 'Listening to "life knowledge": a new research direction in poverty studies', *International Journal of Social Welfare*, no 14, pp 99-106.

Krumer-Nevo, M. and Benjamin, O. (2008) 'Critical poverty knowledge: Contesting othering and social distancing', *Current Sociology*, Vol 58, pp 693-714.

Lambie, K. (2011) *The Trussell Trust Foodbank Network: Exploring the growth of Foodbanks across the UK*, Coventry: Coventry University (www.trusselltrust.org/resources/documents/Our%20work/Lambie-%282011%29-The-Trussell-Trust-Foodbank-Network---Exploring-the-Growth-of-Foodbanks-Across-the-UK.pdf).

Laming, Lord (2003) T*he Victoria Climbie inquiry*, London: Stationery Office.

Lane, R. (2009) 'Self-reliance and empathy: The enemies of poverty – and of the poor', *Qualitative Health Research*, vol 19, no 3, pp 297-310.

Larm, P., Hodgins, S., Larsson, A., Molero Samuelson, Y. and Tengstrom, A. (2008) 'Long-term outcomes of adolescents treated for substance misuse', *Drug and Alcohol Dependence*, Vol 96, no 1-2, pp 79-89.

Levinas, R. (2012) *There may be trouble ahead: What we know about those 120,000 'troubled' families*, Policy Response Series no 3, ESRC Grant RES-060-25-0052, www.poverty.ac.uk/policy-response-working-papers-families-social-policy-life-chances-children-parenting-uk-government

Lewis, O. (1968) *A study of slum culture*, New York: Random House.

Lipsky, M. (1980) *Street-level bureaucracy: The dilemmas of individuals in public service*, New York: Russell Sage Foundation.

Lister, R. (2004) *Poverty*, Cambridge: Polity Press.

Loopstra-Masters, R. and Tarasuk, V. (2012) 'Seeing community gardens, community kitchens and good food box programs through the eyes of low income, food insecure families in Toronto', The Ontario Public Health Convention 2012, University of Toronto.

Lowndes, V. and Pratchett, L. (2012) 'Local governance under the Coalition government: Austerity, localism and the "Big Society"', *Local Government Studies*, vol 38, no 1, pp 21-40.

Lyons, K., Manion, K. and Carlsen, M. (2006) *International perspectives on social work: Global conditions and local practice*, Basingstoke: Palgrave.

McDonald, A. (2010) *Social work with older people*, Cambridge: Polity Press.

Macmillan, L. (2011) 'Measuring the intergenerational correlation of worklessness', Bristol Institute of Public Affairs, Mimeo in S. Harkness, P. Gregg and L. Macmillan (2012) *Poverty: The role of institutions, behaviours and culture*, York: Joseph Rowntree Trust.

Macpherson, W. (1999) *The Stephen Lawrence Inquiry: Report of an Inquiry by Sir William Macpherson of Cluny*, London: HMSO.

McCarthy, K. (2012) *Food Banks in Hampshire*, Winchester: Hampshire Community Action.

McKendrick, J. (2012) *Writing and talking about poverty*, Briefing Paper 26, Edinburgh: The Scottish Government (www.scotland.gov.uk/Resource/Doc/1031/0112468.pdf).

McLaughlin, K. (2005) 'From ridicule to institutionalisation: Anti-oppression, the state and social work', *Critical Social Policy*, vol 25, no 3, pp 283-305.

Malthus, T.R. ([1806] 1989) *An essay on the principle of population*, vol 2, Cambridge: Cambridge University Press.

Mann, K. (1992) *The making of an English underclass*, Milton Keynes: Open University Press.

Manthorpe. J., Hussein, S. and Stevens, M. (2012) 'Communication with migrant workers: The perspectives of people using care services in England', *Practice: Social Work in Action*, vol 24, no 5, pp 299-314.

Mantle, G. and Backwith, D. (2010) 'Poverty and social work', *British Journal of Social Work*, vol 40, pp 2380-97.

May, T., Duffy, M., Few, B. and Hough, M. (2005) *Understanding drug selling in local communities*, York: Joseph Rowntree Trust.

Mencap (2012) *Welfare reform* (www.mencap.org.uk/news/viewpoint-magazine/features/welfare-reform).

Migration Observatory (2013) *Migration to the UK: Asylum*, Oxford: Oxford University, available: www.migrationobservatory.ox.ac.uk/sites/files/migobs/Briefing%20-%20Migration%20to%20the%20UK%20-%20Asylum.pdf

Millar, M. (2008) 'Anti-oppressiveness: Critical comments on a discourse and its context', *British Journal of Social Work*, vol 38, no 2, pp 362-75.

Mind (2012) *Benefits and welfare: We need your help to campaign for a fairer system* (www.mind.org.uk/assets/0001/2156/B_W_campaign_guide.pdf).

Ministry of Justice (2013) *Transforming rehabilitation – A revolution in the way we manage offenders*, London: The Stationery Office.

Mitchell, J., Parutis, V., Retkute, R. and Danielius, L. (2008) *The impact of low wage employment on workers' health, nutrition and living standards: A case for the London Living Wage*, London: Food Commission.

Moffat, K. (1999) 'Surveillance and government of the welfare recipient', in A. Chambon, A. Irving and L. Epstein (eds) *Reading Foucault for social work*, New York: Columbia University Press, pp 219-247.

Monnickendam, M., Katz, Ch. and Monnickendam, M.S. (2010) 'Social workers serving poor clients: Perceptions of poverty and service policy', *British Journal of Social Work*, vol 40, pp 911-27.

Morrell, G. and Wainwright, S. (2006) *Destitution amongst refugees and asylum seekers in the UK*, Briefing, London: Information Centre about Asylum and Refugees (www.icar.org.uk/6575/briefings/destitution.html).

Mullainathan, S. and Shafir, E. (2013) *Scarcity: Why having too little means so much*, London: Allen Lane.

Munro, E. (2011) *The protection of children online: A brief scoping review to identify vulnerable groups*, London: The Child Wellbeing Centre, Institute of Education.

Munro, E. (2012) *The Munro review of child protection progress report: Moving towards a child-centred system*, London: Department for Education.

Murray, C. (1994) *Underclass: The crisis deepens*, London: Institute of Economic Affairs.

Narayan, D. and Petesch, P. (2002) *Voices of the poor: From many lands*, New York: Oxford University Press for The World Bank.

National Audit Office (2011) *Maintaining the financial stability of UK banks: Update on the support schemes*, HC 676 Session 2010-2011, London: The Stationery Office.

National Centre for Social Research (2010) *ASB family intervention projects: Monitoring and evaluation*, London: Department for Children, Schools and Family.

National Treatment Agency for Substance Misuse (2012) *Drug treatment 2012: Progress made, challenges ahead* (www.nta.nhs.uk).

NHS Information Centre (2012) *Statistics on obesity, physical activity and diet: England*, London: NHS Information Centre, Lifestyle Statistics.

Nelson, M., Erens, B., Bates, B., Church, S. and Boshier, T. (2007) *Low income diet and nutrition survey*, Food Standards Survey, London: The Stationery Office.

Nixon, J., Hunter, C., Part, S., Myers, S., Whittle, S. and Sanderson, D. (2006) *Interim evaluation of rehabilitation projects for families at risk of losing their homes as a result of anti-social behaviour*, London: Office of the Deputy Prime Minister.

Novak, T. (1988) *Poverty and the state*, Milton Keynes: Open University Press.

NSPCC (National Society for the Prevention of Cruelty to Children) (2008) *Poverty and child maltreatment*, Child Protection Research Briefing (www.nspcc.org.uk/inform).

O'Brien, M. (2012) 'Policy summary: Fuel poverty in England, *The Lancet* (http://ukpolicymatters.thelancet.com/?p=1603).

Office of the Children's Commissioner (2011) *'Trying to get by': Consulting with children and young people on poverty* (www.childrenscommissioner.gov.uk).

ONS (Office for National Statistics) (2011) *Internet access quarterly update Q2, Internet users Q2 2011*, UK data, Table 1 (www.ons.gov.uk/ons/publications/re-reference-tables.html?edition=tcm%3A77-226794).

ONS (2013) 'Claimant count and vacancies dataset', available from: www.ons.gov.uk/ons/rel/lms/labour-market-statistics/may-2013/dataset--claimant-count-and-vacancies.html

OSCE (Organization for Security and Co-operation in Europe) (2011) *Report by OSCE special representative and co-ordinator for combating trafficking in human beings, following her visit to the UK, 7-10 March 2011*, www.osce.org/cthb/87013

Oxfam (2009) *Who cares? How best to protect UK care workers employed through agencies and gangmasters from exploitation*, Oxford: Oxfam.

Palmer, G., MacInnes, T. and Kenway, P. (2006) *Monitoring poverty and social exclusion in Scotland*, York: Joseph Rowntree Foundation.

Park, A., Clery, E., Curtice, J., Phillips, M. and Utting, D. (2012) *British social attitudes 29*, London: National Centre for Social Research.

Parrott, L. (2010) *Values and ethics in social work practice* (revised edn), London: Sage Publications.

Parrott, L., Jacobs, G. and Roberts, D. (2008) *Stress and resilience factors in parents with mental health problems and their children*, London: Social Care Institute for Excellence.

Parton, N. and O'Byrne, P. (2000) *Constructive social work: Towards a new practice*, London: Macmillan.

Payne, M. (2000) *Anti-bureaucratic social work*, Birmingham: Venture Press.

Pierson, J. (2011) *Understanding social work: History and context*, Maidenhead: Open University Press.

Pinter, I. (2012) *I don't feel human: Experiences of destitution among young refugees and migrants*, London: The Children's Society.

Polanyi, K. (1957) *The great transformation*, Boston, MA: Beacon Press.

Poverty Site, The (2012) *Lacking consumer durables* (www.poverty.org.uk/11/index.shtml).

Poverty Site, The (2013) 'What the indicators show: Disability' (www.poverty. org.uk/summary/disability.htm).

Powell, F. (2001) *The politics of social work*, London: Sage Publications.

Pugh, R. (1996) *Effective language in health and social work*, London: Chapman & Hall Publishing.

Pugh, R. and Gould, N. (2000) 'Globalisation, social work and social welfare', *European Journal of Social Work*, vol 3, no 2, pp 123-38.

Rainville, B. and Brink, S. (2001) *Food insecurity in Canada, 1998-1999*, Applied Research Branch Strategic Policy, Québec: Human Resources Development Canada.

Ravensbergen, F. and VanderPlaat, M. (2010) 'Barriers to citizen participation: the missing voices of people living with low income', *Community Development Journal*, vol 45, no 4, pp 389-403.

Reamer, A. (2005) 'Documentation in social work: Evolving ethical and risk-management standards', *Social Work*, vol 50, no 4, pp 325-34.

Ref Department of Health (2000) *Framework for the assessment of children in need and their families*, London: Stationery Office.

Refugee Council (2012) *Asylum statistics, September 2012* (www.refugeecouncil. org.uk/assets/0001/5778/Asylum_Statistics__Aug_2012.pdf)

Refugee Media Action Group (2006) *Seeking asylum: A report on the living conditions of asylum seekers in London*, London: Migrants Resource Centre.

Resolution Foundation (2012) *Gaining from growth: The final report of the Commission on Living Standards*, London: Resolution Foundation.

Resolution Foundation (2013) *Home Truths*, www.resolutionfoundation.org/ publications/home-truths-how-affordable-housing-britains-ordina/

Reynolds, S. (2010) *Your inflexible friend: The cost of living without cash*, Asylum Support Partnership (http://stillhumanstillhere.files.wordpress.com/2009/01/ your-inflexible-friend-the-cost-of-living-without-cash.pdf).

Riches, G. (2002) 'Food Banks and food security: Welfare reform, human rights and social policy. Lessons from Canada?', *Social Policy & Administration*, vol 36, no 6, pp 648-63.

Riches, G. (2011) 'Thinking and acting outside the charitable food box: hunger and the right to food in rich societies', *Development in Practice*, vol 21, nos 4-5, pp 768-75.

Ridge, T. (2009) *Living with poverty: A review of the literature on children's and families' experiences of poverty*, DWP Research Report No 594, London: The Stationery Office.

Rogowski, S. (2011) 'Managers, managerialism and social work with children and families: The deformation of a profession?', *Practice: Social Work in Action*, vol 23, no 3, pp 157-67.

Rose, N. (1996a) 'The death of the social? Reconfiguring the territory of government', *Economy and Society*, vol 25, no 3, pp 327-56.

Rothstein, B. (1998) *Just institutions matter: The moral and political logic of the universal welfare state*, Cambridge: Cambridge University Press.

Rowntree, B.S. (1901) *Poverty: A study of town life*, London: Macmillan.

Rowntree, B.S. (1941) *Poverty and progress: A second social survey of York*, London: Longman.

Roxborough, R. (2011) 'Incapacity Benefit/Employment Support Allowance migration pilots', *Journal of Poverty and Social Justice*, vol 19, no 2, pp 181-3.

Royal College of Physicians (2005) *Food poverty and health: Briefing statement*, London: Royal College of Physicians.

Rutter, M. and Madge, N. (1976) *Cycles of disadvantage*, London: Heinemann.

Sakamoto, I. and Pitner, R. (2005) 'Use of critical consciousness in anti-oppressive social work practice: Disentangling power dynamics at personal and structural levels', *British Journal of Social Work*, no 35, pp 435-52.

Samani-Radia, D. and McCarthy, H.D. (2011) 'Comparison of children's body fatness between two contrasting income groups: contribution of height difference', *International Journal of Obesity*, vol 35, pp 128-33.

Sandel, M. (2012) *What money can't buy: The moral limits of markets*, London: Allen Lane.

Save the Children (2012a) *Ending child poverty: Ensuring Universal Credit helps working mums*, London: Save the Children Fund.

Save the Children (2012b) *Child poverty in 2012: It shouldn't happen here*, London: Save the Children.

Save the Children (2012c) 'Rising Energy Costs: The impact on low-income families', Save the Children, www.savethechildren.org.uk/resources/online-library/rising-energy-costs-impact-low-income-families

SCIE (Social Care Institute for Excellence) (2010) *Good practice in social care with refugees and asylum seekers*, Workforce Development, SCIE Guide 37, London: SCIE (www.scie.org.uk/publications/guides/guide37/files/guide37.pdf).

Schorr, A. (1992) *The Personal Social Services: An outsider's view*, York: Joseph Rowntree Foundation.

Scottish Executive (2006) *Good practice guidance for working with children and families affected by substance misuse: Getting our priorities right*, Edinburgh: Scottish Executive.

Scourfield, P. (2007) 'Are there reasons to be worried about the "caretelization" of residential care?', *Critical Social Policy*, vol 27, no 2, pp 155-80.

Scourfield, P. (2011) 'Caretelization revisited and the lessons of Southern Cross', *Critical Social Policy*, vol 32, no 1, pp 137-48.

Seddon, T. (2006) 'Drugs, crime and social exclusion: Social context and social theory in British drugs – Crime research', *British Journal of Criminology*, vol 46, pp 680-703.

Sewpaul, V. (2005) 'Global standards: promise and pitfalls for re-inscribing social work into civil society', *International Journal of Social Welfare*, vol 14, pp 210-17.

Shaw, A., Egan, J. and Gillespie, M. (2007) *Drugs and poverty: A literature review*, Glasgow: Scottish Association of Alcohol and Drug Action Teams.

Shildrick, T., MacDonald, R., Furlong, A., Roden, J. and Crow, R. (2012) *Are 'cultures of worklessness' passed down the generations?*, York: Joseph Rowntree Trust.

Shutes, I. (2012) 'Migrant care workers in ageing societies', Research Highlights, *Journal of Poverty and Social Justice*, vol 20, no 1, pp 97-111.

Shutes, I. and Chiatti, C. (2012) 'Migrant labour and the marketisation of care for older people: The employment of migrant care workers by families and service providers', *Journal of European Social Policy*, vol 22, no 4, pp 392-405.

Sidebotham, P., Heron, J. and Goulding, J. (2002) 'Child maltreatment in the "Children of the Nineties": deprivation, class, and social networks in a UK sample', *Child Abuse & Neglect*, vol 26, no 12, pp 1243-301.

Smale, G., Tuson, G., Behal, N. and Marsh, P. (1993) *Empowerment, assessment, care management and the skilled worker*, London: National Institute for Social Work.

Smart, K. and Fullegar, S. (2008) *The destitution tally: An indication of the extent of destitution among asylum seekers and refugees*, London: Asylum Support.

Social Exclusion Task Force (2007) *Families at risk: Background on families with multiple disadvantages*, London: Cabinet Office.

Spicer, N. (2008) 'Places of exclusion and inclusion: Asylum-seeker and refugee experiences of neighbourhoods in the UK', *Journal of Ethnic and Migration Studies*, vol 34, no 3, pp 491-510.

SSAC (Social Security Advisory Committee) (2012) *Universal Credit and conditionality*, SSAC Occasional Paper No 9, London: SSAC.

Stanley, N., Austerberry, H., Bilson, A., Farrelly, N., Hargreaves, K., Hussein, S., Ingold, A., Manthorpe, J., Ridley, J. and Strange, V. (2012) 'Establishing social work practices in England: The early evidence', *British Journal of Social Work*, Advanced Access, published 15 July, pp 1-17.

Stedman Jones, G. (1984) *Outcast London: A study in the relationship between classes in Victorian society*, Harmondsworth: Penguin.

Stevenson, S. (2013) 'Food Security Policy: A review of literature and synthesis of key recommendations for Toi Te Ora - Public Health Service', www.ttophs.govt.nz/vdb/document/741

Stiller, S. and van Kersbergen, K. (2005) 'Welfare state research and the (in)dependent variable problem: What to explain and how to explain?', Paper presented at ESPANet Conference, Fribourg, Swizerland, 22-24 September.

Strier, R. and Binyamin, S. (2010) 'Developing anti-oppressive services for the poor: A theoretical and organisational rationale', *British Journal of Social Work*, vol 40, pp 1908-26.

SWAN (Social Work Action Network) (2013) www.socialworkfuture.org

Taylor-Gooby, P. (2011) *Squaring the public policy circle: Managing a mismatch between demands and resources*, London: The British Academy.

Thompson, E.P. (1968) *The making of the English working class*, London: Penguin.

Thompson, N. (2001) *Anti-Discriminatory Practice*, Basingstoke, Palgrave/Macmillan

Townend, L. (2010) 'The moralizing of obesity: A new name for an old sin?', *Critical Social Policy*, vol 29, no 2, pp 171-90.

Townsend, I. (2004) *Poverty measures and targets*, House of Commons Research Paper, 04/23, London: Hansard.

Townsend, P. (1979) *Poverty in the UK*, Harmondsworth: Penguin.

Tronto, J. (2010) 'Creating caring institutions: Politics, plurality, and purpose', *Ethics and Social Welfare*, vol 4, no 2, pp 158-71.

Trussell Trust (2012) The Trussell Trust's UK foodbank network (http://www.trusselltrust.org/resources/documents/Press/General_Foodbank_Appeal2012_NORDO.pdf).

TUC (Trades Union Congress) (2013) 'Rise in zero hours contracts a "worrying trend" says TUC', press release 3rd July (www.tuc.org.uk/workplace/tuc-22328-f0.cfm).

TUC/YouGov (2013) 'Support for benefit cuts dependent on ignorance, TUC-commissioned poll finds', 4 January, Press release (www.tuc.org.uk/social/tuc-21796-f0.cfm).

Underlid, K. (2005) 'Poverty and experiences of social devaluation: A qualitative interview study of 25 long-standing recipients of social security payments', *Scandinavian Journal of Psychology*, vol 46, pp 273-83.

Underlid, K. (2007) 'Poverty and experiences of insecurity: A qualitative study of 25 long-standing recipients of social security', *International Journal of Social Welfare*, vol 16, no 1, pp 65-74.

Ungar, M., Brown, M., Liebenberg, L., Othman, R., Kwong, W.M., Armstrong, M. and Gilgun, J. (2004) 'Unique pathways to resilience across cultures', *Adolescence*, vol 42, no 166, pp 287-310.

UNISON (2008) *10 reasons to oppose social work practices* (www.unison.org.uk/acrobat/A7623A.pdf).

US Department Of Health and Human Services (2012) *National Center for Health Statistics. Prevalence of obesity in the United States, 2009-2010. Jan 2012* (www.cdc.gov/nchs/data/databriefs/db82.htm).

Veit-Wilson, J. (1986) 'Paradigms of poverty: a rehabilitation of R.S. Rowntree', *Journal of Social Policy*, vol 15, pp 69-99.

Walker, J., Crawford, K. and Taylor, F. (2008) 'Listening to children: gaining a perspective of the experiences of poverty and social exclusion from children and young people of single-parent families', *Health & Social Care in the Community*, vol 16, no 4, pp 429-36.

Wanless, D. (2004) *Securing good health for the whole population: Final report*, London: HM Treasury.

Wastell, D., White, S., Broadhurst, K., Hall, C. and Peckover, S. (2009) 'The chiasmus of design: paradoxical outcomes in the e-Government reform of the UK children's service', in G. Dhillon, B.C. Stahl and R. Baskerville (eds) *IFIP advances in information and communication technology*, Boston, MA: Springer-Boston, pp 257-72.

White, M. (2007) 'Food access and obesity', *Obesity Review*, no 8, Supplement 1, pp 99-107.

White, S., Hall, C. and Peckover, S. (2009) 'The descriptive tyranny of the common assessment framework: Technologies of categorization and professional practice in child welfare', *British Journal of Social Work*, vol 39, no 7, pp 1197-217.

Wiggan, J. (2012) 'Telling stories of 21st century welfare: The UK Coalition Government and the neo-liberal discourse of worklessness and dependency', *Critical Social Policy*, vol 32, no 3, pp 383-405.

Wilkinson, M. (2012) 'Out of sight, out of mind: the exploitation of migrant workers in 21st-century Britain', *Journal of Poverty and Social Justice*, vol 20, no 1, pp 13-21.

Wilkinson, R. and Pickett, K. (2010) *The spirit level: Why equality is better for everyone*, London: Penguin.

Wilks, T. (2012) *Advocacy and social work practice*, Maidenhead: Open University Press.

Williams, C. and Parrott, L. (2012) 'Anti-racism and predominantly "white areas": Local and national referents in the search for race equality in social work education', *British Journal of Social Work*, Advanced Publication, 12 July.

Williams, F. (2004) 'What matters is who works: commentary on the Green Paper Every Child Matters', *Critical Social Policy*, Vol 24, No 3, pp 406-427.

Wilson, A. and Beresford, P. (2000) '"Anti-oppressive practice": emancipation or appropriation?', *British Journal of Social Work*, vol 5, no 30, pp 553-73.

Wilton, R. (2003) 'Poverty and mental health: A qualitative study of residential care facility tenants', *Community Mental Health Journal*, vol 39, no 2, pp 139-42.

Wolfensberger, W. (1992) *A brief introduction to social role valorization as a high-order concept for structuring human services* (2nd revised edn), Syracuse, NY: Training Institute for Human Service Planning, Leadership and Change Agentry (Syracuse University).

Women's Budget Group (2008) *Women and poverty: Experiences, empowerment and engagement*, York: Joseph Rowntree Trust.

Woodroofe, K. (1962) *From charity to social work*, London: RKP.

Wright, F. (2012) 'Social work practice with unaccompanied asylum-seeking young people facing removal', *British Journal of Social Work*, Advanced Access, published 23 November, pp 1-18.

Yeates, N. (2012) 'Global care chains: a state-of-the-art review and future directions in care transnationalization research', *Global Networks*, vol 12, no 2, pp 135-54.

Young, H., Grundy, E. and Jitlal, M. (2006) *Characteristics of care providers and care receivers over time*, York: Joseph Rowntree Trust.

Index